Debbie Bliss
baby and toddler knits

20 classic patterns for clothes, blankets, hats, and bootees

CICO BOOKS

LONDON NEW YORK

For Raewyn, Hans, Max and Sam

This edition published in 2021 by CICO Books
an imprint of Ryland Peters & Small Ltd
20–21 Jockey's Fields   341 E 116th Street
London WC1R 4BW   New York NY 10012

www.rylandpeters.com

1 3 5 7 9 10 8 6 4 2

First published in 2002

Patterns in this book are taken from *Cotton Knits for All Seasons*, also published in 2002
by CICO Books

A CIP catalog record for this book is available from
the Library of Congress and the British Library.

ISBN: 978 1 78249 890 2

Printed in China

Edited by Kate Haxell
Photography by Craig Fordham
Styling by Sammi Bell
Designed by Sara Kidd
Book design conceived by Janet James
Patterns checked by Marilyn Wilson
Illustrations by Stephen Dew and Kate Simunek

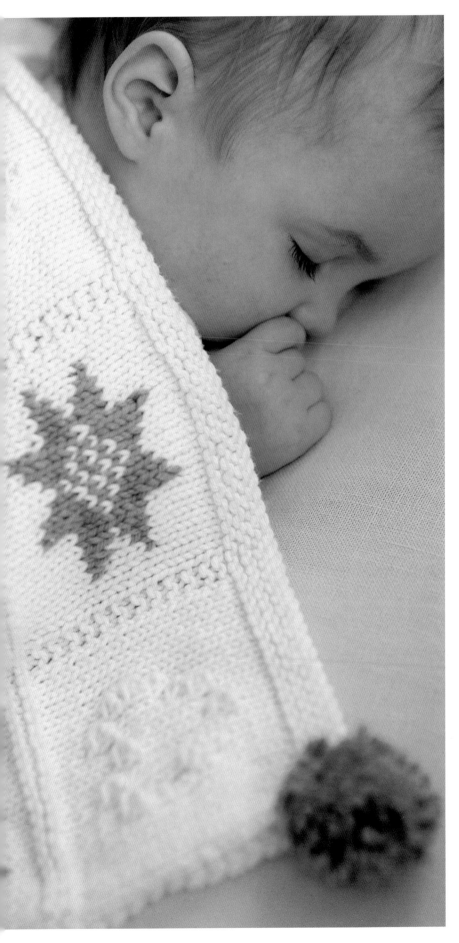

contents

INTRODUCTION

Baby and Toddler Knits has given me a great opportunity to design a collection of knits that young children will love to wear. There are over 20 designs, ranging from pretty summer cardigans to cable knit sweaters, sporty knits for boys and a snowflake and heart baby throw.

Many of the projects use cotton, the perfect material for kids as it is cool in the summer and warm in the winter, making it a great all-year-round yarn. The pure cotton double knitting yarn knits up quickly and smoothly to create colourful motif knits, and clearly shows the stitch detail in the textured knits. I have also used my ever-popular baby cashmerino mix – which combines the softness of cashmere with essential wash-and-wear properties – in a modern layette, a pretty cardigan, and a simple striped top.

There are designs here for a range of knitting skills, but the emphasis is on simple shapes in stylish knits. However, for less experienced knitters who want to expand their skills, there are step-by-step diagrams for colourwork and cables.

Debbie Bliss

EMBROIDERED dress

A simple, sleeveless dress with mock pleats is embellished with a swag of embroidery on the yoke. This design is not only perfect as a summer dress, but also works well as a winter pinafore, worn over a long-sleeved top.

Materials

Debbie Bliss Cotton DK (100% cotton; 84m/91yd per 50g/1¾oz ball) DK (light worsted) weight yarn:
  7(8:9) balls of shade Mint
Pair each of 3.25mm (US 3) and 4mm (US 6) knitting needles
Small amounts of yarn in five colours for embroidery (see page 90)

Measurements

To fit ages	1	2	3	years.
Actual measurements				
Chest	51	56	61	cm
	20	22	24	in
Length to shoulder	44	49	53	cm
	17½	19¼	21	in

Tension

20 sts and 28 rows to 10cm/4in square over st st using 4mm (US 6) needles.

Abbreviations

See page 95.

BACK

With 4mm (US 6) needles cast on 122(134:146) sts.
1st rib row K4, p5, ★ k7, p5; rep from ★ to last 5 sts, k5.
2nd rib row P5, k5, ★ p7, k5; rep from ★ to last 4 sts, p4.
These 2 rows set the rib patt.
Work a further 8(18:28) rows.
Dec row (right side) K4, p2, p2tog, p1, ★ k7, p2, p2tog, p1; rep from ★ to last 5 sts, k5.
Work 9 rows rib as set.
Dec row (right side) K4, p4,★ k3, skpo, k2, p4; rep from ★ to last 5 sts, k5.
Work 9 rows rib as set.
Dec row (right side) K4, p1, p2tog, p1,★ k6, p1, p2tog, p1; rep from ★ to last 5 sts, k5.
Work 9 rows rib as set.
Dec row (right side) K4, p3, ★ k2, skpo, k2, p3; rep from ★ to last 5 sts, k2, skpo, k1.
Work 9 rows rib as set.
Dec row (right side) K4, p1, p2tog, ★ k5, p1, p2tog; rep from ★ to last 4 sts, k4.
Work 9 rows rib as set.
Dec row (right side) K1, skpo, k1, p2, ★ k1, skpo, k2, p2; rep from ★ to last 4 sts, k4.
Work 9 rows rib as set.

Dec row (right side) K3, ★ p2tog, k4; rep from ★ to end. 53(58:63) sts.
Cont in rib as set until back measures 28(32:36)cm/11(12½:14¼)in from cast on edge, ending with a wrong side row.
Beg with a k row work 4(6:8) rows st st.

Shape armholes

Next row Cast off 3 sts at the beg of the next 2 rows.
Dec one st at each end of the next 2 rows then every foll alt row until 39(44:49) sts rem.
Work straight until back measures 43(48:52)cm/17(18¾:20½)in from cast on edge, ending with a wrong side row.

Shape back neck

Next row K8(10:11), turn and work on these sts for first side of neck.
Work 1 row.
Next row K6(8:9), k2 tog.
Work 1 row.
Cast off rem 7(9:10) sts.
With right side facing, slip centre 23(24:27) sts on a holder, rejoin yarn to rem sts and k to end.
Work 1 row.
Next row Skpo, k to end.
Work 1 row.
Cast off rem 7(8:9) sts.

FRONT

Work as given for Back until 14(16:18) rows less have been worked than Back to shoulder shaping, ending with a wrong side row.

Shape neck

Next row K12(14:15), turn and work on these sts for first side of neck.
Work 1 row.
Next row K10(12:13), k2tog.
Work 1 row.
Rep last 2 rows until 8(10:11) sts rem.
Cont straight until front measures same as Back to shoulder shaping, ending with a wrong side row.
Cast off.
With right side facing, slip centre 15(16:19) sts on a holder, rejoin yarn to rem sts and work as given for left side reversing shapings.

NECKBAND

Join left shoulder seam.

With 3.25mm (US 3) needles and right side facing, pick up and k14(15:16) sts down left front neck, k15(16:19) sts from front neck holder, pick up and k14(15:16) sts up right front neck, 4 sts down right back neck, k23(24:27) sts from back neck holder, pick up and k4 sts up left back neck. 74(78:86) sts.

1st row K2, ★ p2, k2; rep from ★ to end.
2nd row P2, ★ k2, p2; rep from ★ to end.
Rep the last 2 rows once more.
Cast off in rib.

ARMBANDS (BOTH ALIKE)

Join right shoulder seam.

With 3.25 mm (US 3) needles and right side facing, pick up and k62(70:78) sts around armhole edge.

Work 4 rows in rib as given for Neckband.
Cast off in rib.

MAKE UP

Using satin stitch, lazy daisy and French knots, work embroidery on front yoke as shown in diagram above and on page 90.

Join side seams.

BABY BOBBLE jacket

This textured cardigan is knitted in a cashmere mix in a soft, dusky pink. The bobble and cable pattern is echoed in the neat garter stitch borders with bobble detailing.

Materials

Debbie Bliss Baby Cashmerino (55% wool, 33% acrylic, 12% cashmere; 125m/137yd per 50g/1¾oz ball) light DK (sport) weight yarn:
  5 (5:6) balls of shade Mink
Pair each of 2.75mm (US 2) and 3.25mm (US 3) knitting needles
Cable needle
5 buttons

Measurements

To fit ages	3-6	6-9	9-12	months.
Actual measurements				
Chest	60	63	66	cm
	23½	24¾	26	in
Length to shoulder	24	26	28	cm
	9½	10¼	11	in
Sleeve length	14	16	18	cm
	5½	6¼	7	in

Tension

25 sts and 34 rows to 10cm/4in square over st st using 3.25mm (US 3) needles.

Abbreviations

Tw4Rb – slip next st onto cable needle and leave at back, k1b, p1, k1b, then p1 from cable needle.
Tw4Lb – slip next 3 sts onto cable needle and leave at front, p1, then k1b, p1, k1b, from cable needle.
Mb – work k1, p1, k1, p1, k1, into next st, turn, p5, turn, k5, pass 2nd, 3rd, 4th and 5th st over first and off the needle.
C4F – slip next 2 sts onto cable needle and leave at front, k2, then k2, from cable needle.
See also pages 88 and 95.

PATT PANEL

(worked over 23(25:25) sts)
1st row (right side) P7(8:8), Tw4Rb, k1b, Tw4Lb, p7(8:8).
2nd row K7(8:8), p1, [k1, p1] 4 times, k7(8:8).
3rd row P6(7:7), Tw4Rb, k1, k1b, k1, Tw4Lb, p6(7:7).
4th row K6(7:7), p1, k1, p1, [k2, p1] twice, k1, p1, k6(7:7).
5th row P5(6:6), Tw4Rb, k2, k1b, k2, Tw4Lb, p5(6:6).
6th row K5(6:6), p1, k1, p2, k2, p1, k2, p2, k1, p1, k5(6:6).
7th row P4(5:5), Tw4Rb, k1b, [k2, k1b] twice, Tw4Lb, p4(5:5).
8th row K4(5:5), p1, [k1, p1] twice, [k2, p1] twice, [k1, p1] twice, k4(5:5).
9th row P3(4:4), Tw4Rb, k1, k1b, [k2, k1b] twice, k1, Tw4Lb, p3(4:4).
10th row K3(4:4), p1, k1, p1, [k2, p1] 4 times, k1, p1, k3(4:4).
11th row P2(3:3), Tw4Rb, k2, [k1b, k2] 3 times, Tw4Lb, p2(3:3).
12th row K2(3:3), p1, k1, p1, k3, p1, [k2, p1] twice, k3, p1, k1, p1, k2(3:3).
13th row P2(3:3), k1b, p1, k1b, k3, Mb, [k2, Mb] twice, k3, k1b, p1, k1b, p2(3:3).
14th row K2(3:3), p1, k1, p1, k3, p1b, [k2, p1b] twice, k3, p1, k1, p1, k2(3:3).
15th row P2(3:3), k1b, p1, k1b, p3, k1b, p1, [k1b] 3 times, p1, k1b, p3, k1b, p1, k1b, p2(3:3).
16th row K8(9:9), p1, k1, p3, k1, p1, k8(9:9).
These 16 rows form the patt and are repeated throughout.

BACK

With 2.75mm (US 2) needles cast on 87(91:97) sts.

K 3 rows to form garter st hem.

Next row K4(3:3) ★ Mb, k5; rep from ★ to last 5(4:4) sts, Mb, k4(3:3).

K 3 rows, inc one st at end of last row on 1st and 2nd sizes only. 88(92:97) sts.

Change to 3.25mm (US 3) needles.

1st row K15(15:17), work across 1st row of patt panel, k12(12:13), work across 1st row of patt panel, k15(15:17).

2nd row K3(3:4), p4, k4(4:5), p4, work across 2nd row of patt panel, p4, k4(4:5), p4, work across 2nd row of patt panel, p4, k4(4:5), p4, k3(3:4).

3rd row K3(3:4), C4F, k4(4:5), C4F, work across 3rd row of patt panel, C4F, k4(4:5), C4F, work across 3rd row of patt panel, C4F, k4(4:5), C4F, k3(3:4).

4th row K3(3:4), p4, k4(4:5), p4, work across 4th row of patt panel, p4, k4(4:5), p4, work across 4th row of patt panel, p4, k4(4:5), p4, k3(3:4).

These 4 rows **set** the position for patt panels and form garter st and cable panels.

Cont in patt until back measures 24(26:28)cm/9½(10¼:11)in from cast on edge, ending with a wrong side row.

Shape shoulders

Cast off 14(14:15) sts at beg of next 2 rows and 14(15:16) sts on foll 2 rows.

Cast off rem 32(34:35) sts.

LEFT FRONT

With 2.75mm (US 2) needles cast on 46(48:50) sts.

K 3 rows.

Next row K4(3:3) ★ Mb, k5; rep from ★ to last 6(9:5) sts, Mb, k5(8:4).

K 3 rows.

Change to 3.25mm (US 3) needles.

1st row K15(15:17), work across 1st row of patt panel, k8.

2nd row K4, p4, work across 2nd row of patt panel, p4, k4(4:5), p4, k3(3:4).

3rd row K3(3:4), C4F, k4(4:5), C4F, work across 3rd row of patt panel, C4F, k4.

4th row K4, p4, work across 4th row of patt

panel, p4, k4(4:5), p4, k3(3:4).

These 4 rows **set** the position for patt panels and form garter st and cable panels.

Cont in patt until front measures 20(22:24)cm/8(8¾:9½)in from cast on edge, ending with a wrong side row.

Shape neck

Next row Patt to last 8 sts, leave these sts on a safety-pin, turn and work on rem sts.

Dec one st at neck edge on every row until 28(29:31) sts rem.

Work straight until front measures same as Back to shoulder shaping, ending at side edge.

Shape shoulder

Cast off 14(14:15) sts at beg of next row.

Work 1 row.

Cast off rem 14(15:16) sts.

Mark positions for buttons: the first 3cm/1¼in from cast on edge, the fifth 1cm/½in from neck edge, the rem three spaced evenly between.

RIGHT FRONT

Work buttonholes to match markers as folls:

Buttonhole row (right side) K1, k2 tog, yf, k1, patt to end.

With 2.75mm (US 2) needles cast on 46(48:50) sts.

K 3 rows.

Next row K5(8:4) ★ Mb, k5; rep from ★ to last 5(4:4) sts, Mb, k4(3:3).

K 3 rows.

Change to 3.25mm (US 3) needles.

1st row K8, work across 1st row of patt panel, k15(15:17).

2nd row K3(3:4), p4, k4(4:5), p4, work across 2nd row of patt panel, p4, k4.

3rd row K4, C4F, work across 3rd row of patt panel, C4F, k4(4:5), C4F, k3(3:4).

4th row K3(3:4), p4, k4(4:5), p4, work across 4th row of patt panel, p4, k4.

These 4 rows **set** the position for patt panels and form garter st and cable panels.

Cont in patt until front measures 20(22:24)cm/8(8¾:9½)in from cast on edge, ending with a right side row.

Shape neck

Next row Patt 8 sts, leave these sts on a safety-pin, patt to end.

Dec one st at neck edge on every row until 28(29:31) sts rem.

Work straight until front measures same as Back to shoulder shaping, ending at side edge.

Shape shoulder

Cast off 14(14:15) sts at beg of
next row.

Work 1 row.

Cast off rem 14(15:16) sts.

SLEEVES

With 2.75mm (US 2) needles
cast on 41(45:49) sts.

K 3 rows.

Next row K5(4:3) ★ Mb, k5; rep
from ★ to last 6(5:4) sts, Mb,
k5(4:3).

K 3 rows.

Change to 3.25mm (US 3)
needles.

1st row K9(10:12), work across
1st row of patt panel, k9(10:12).

2nd row P1(2:3), k4(4:5), p4,
work across 2nd row of patt
panel, p4, k4(4:5), p1(2:3).

3rd row K1(2:3), k4(4:5), C4F, work across 3rd row of patt
panel, C4F, k4(4:5), k1(2:3).

4th row P1(2:3), k4(4:5), p4, work across 4th row of patt
panel, p4, k4(4:5), p1(2:3).

These 4 rows **set** the position for patt panels and form garter
st and cable panels.

Cont in patt as set **at the same time** inc one st at each end
of the next and every foll 4th row until there are 57(63:71)
sts, working first 3(2:1) sts into cable panel and the rem sts in
reverse st st.

Cont straight until sleeve measures 14(16:18)cm/5½(6¼:7)in
from cast on edge, ending with a wrong side row.

Cast off.

COLLAR

Join shoulder seams.

With right side facing using 2.75mm (US 2) needles, slip
8 sts from safety-pin onto a needle, pick up and k12 sts up
right front, 29 sts from back neck, pick up and k12 sts down
left side of front neck, k8 from safety-pin. 69 sts.

Next row K to end.

Beg with a p row cont in st st with 4 sts in garter st at
each end.

Next 2 rows Work to last 15 sts, turn.

Next 2 rows Work to last 10 sts, turn.

Work to end.

Next row Cast off 2 sts, k to end.

Next row Cast off 2 sts, k next 3 sts, p to last 4 sts, k4.

Next row K to end.

Next row K4, p to last 4 sts, k4.

Rep the last 2 rows once more.

Next row K2, Mb, k to last 3 sts, Mb, k2.

Next row K4, p to last 4 sts, k4.

Rep the last 6 rows once more.

K 4 rows.

Next row K2, ★ Mb, k5; rep from ★ to last 3
sts, Mb, k2.

K 2 rows

Cast off.

MAKE UP

Sew on sleeves. Join side and sleeve seams.

Sew on buttons.

FLORAL jacket

This is a great jacket for the summer. It can look pretty and dressed-up or sporty and casual. The design would look equally effective worked in lighter, toning shades against a dark background, such as pinks on navy blue.

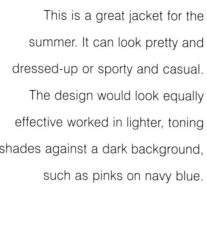

Materials
Debbie Bliss Cotton DK (100% cotton; 84m/91yd per 50g/1¾oz ball) DK (light worsted) weight yarn:
  6(7) balls of shade White (M)
  1 ball each of shades:
  French Navy (A))
  Duck Egg (B)
  Steel Blue (C)
Pair each of 3.25mm (US 3) and 4mm (US 6) knitting needles
7(8) buttons

Measurements

To fit ages	2-3	3-4	years.
Actual measurements			
Chest	78	84	cm
	30¾	33	in
Length to shoulder	31	35	cm
	12¼	13¾	in
Sleeve length	21	24	cm
	8¼	9½	in

Tension
20 sts and 28 rows to 10cm/4in square over st st using 4mm (US 6) needles.

Abbreviations
See page 95.

Note
When working motifs, use separate balls of yarn for each area of colour and twist yarns together on wrong side to avoid holes (see page 86).

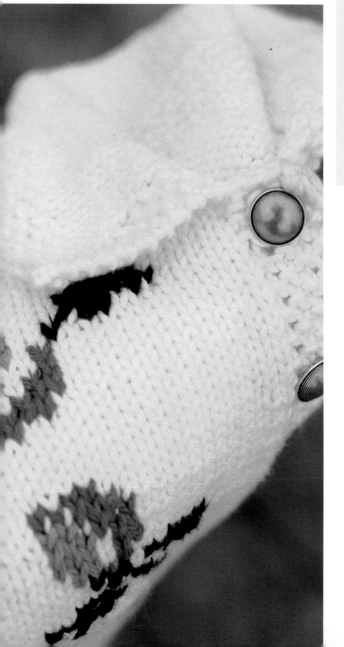

BACK
With 3.25mm (US 3) needles and M cast on 72(78) sts and work moss st hem.
1st row ★ K1, p1; rep from ★ to end.
2nd row ★ P1, k1; rep from ★ to end.
Rep the last 2 rows 3 times more.
Change to 4mm (US 6) needles.
Beg with a k row, work 0(2) rows st st.
1st row K5(7)M, reading chart from right to left, k across 1st row of Chart, k16(18)M, reading chart from left to right, k across 1st row of Chart, k5(7)M.
2nd row P5(7)M, reading chart from right to left, p across 2nd row of Chart, p16(18)M, reading chart from left to right, p across 2nd row of Chart, p5(7)M.
3rd row K5(7)M, reading chart from right to left, k across 3rd row of Chart, k16(18)M, reading chart from left to right, k across 3rd row of Chart, k5(7)M.
4th row P5(7)M, reading chart from right to

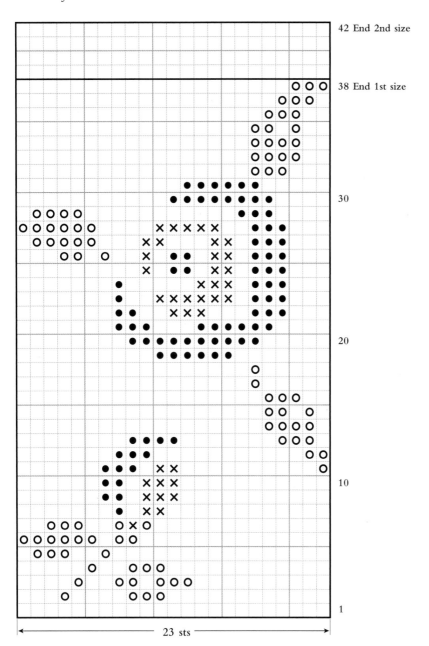

Key

☐	White (M)
○	French Navy (A)
✗	Duck Egg (B)
●	Steel Blue (C)

42 End 2nd size
38 End 1st size
30
20
10
1

← 23 sts →

left, p across 4th row of Chart, p16(18)M,
reading chart from left to right, p across 4th
row of Chart, p5(7)M.
These 4 rows set the 38(42) row patt.
Cont in patt **at the same time** inc one st at
each end of the next every foll 8th row until
there are 80(86) sts.
Work straight until 40(46) rows have been
worked, ending with a wrong side row.

Shape armholes
Cast off 4 sts at beg of next 2 rows.
Cont straight until 76(86) rows have been
worked from top of moss st hem.

Cont in M only.
Work 2(4) rows in st st, then work 6 rows in moss st.

Shape shoulders
Cast off 12(13) sts at beg of next 4 rows.
Leave rem 24(26) sts on a holder.

LEFT FRONT
With 3.25mm (US 3) needles and M cast on 38(40) sts.
Work 8 rows moss st as given for Back, inc 0(1) st at centre
of last row. 38(41) sts.
Change to 4mm (US 6) needles.

2nd size only

Next row K to last 5 sts, moss st 5.

Next row Moss st 5, p to end.

Both sizes

1st row K5(7)M, reading chart from right to left, k across 1st row of Chart, k5(6)M, moss st 5.

2nd row Moss st 5, p5(6), reading chart from left to right, p across 2nd row of Chart, p5(7)M.

3rd row K5(7)M, reading chart from right to left, k across 3rd row of Chart, k5(6)M, moss st 5.

4th row Moss st 5, p5(6)M, reading chart from left to right, p across 4th row of Chart, p5(7)M.

These 4 rows set the 38(42) row patt.

Cont in patt to match Back, **at the same time** inc one st at side edge of the next and every foll 8th row until there are 42(45) sts.

Work straight until 40(46) rows have been worked, ending with a wrong side row.

Shape armhole

Cast off 4 sts at beg of next row.

Cont straight until 70(80) rows have been worked, ending with a wrong side row.

Shape neck

Next row Patt to last 5 sts, turn, leave rem sts on a safety-pin.

Cast off 3 sts at beg of next row and 2(3) sts at beg of foll alt row.

Dec one st at neck edge on every row until 24(26) sts rem.

Work 6 rows moss st.

Shape shoulder

Cast off 12(13) sts at beg of next row.

Patt 1 row.

Cast off rem 12(13) sts.

Mark positions for buttons on left front, the first to come on the 3rd row from cast on edge, the last to come 2 rows below neck shaping, and rem 3(4) spaced evenly between.

RIGHT FRONT

With 3.25mm (US 3) needles and M cast on
38(40) sts.
Work 2 rows moss st as given for Back.
Buttonhole row Moss st 2, work 2 tog, yon,
moss st 1, patt to end.
Work 5 rows moss st.
Change to 4mm (US 6) needles.

2nd size only
Next row Moss st 5, k to end.
Next row P to last 5 sts, moss st 5.

Both sizes
1st row Moss st 5, k5(6)M, reading chart from left to right, k
across 1st row of Chart, k5(7)M.
2nd row P5(7)M, reading chart from right to left, p across

2nd row of Chart, p5(6)M, moss st 5.

3rd row Moss st 5, k5(6)M, reading chart from left to right, k across 3rd row of Chart, k5(7)M.

4th row P5(7)M, reading chart from right to left, p across 4th row of Chart, p5(6)M, moss st 5.

These 4 rows set the 38(42) row patt.

Complete to match Left Front, reversing shapings and making buttonholes as before to match markers.

SLEEVES

With 3.25mm (US 3) needles and M cast on 38(42) sts.

Work 11 rows moss st as given for Back.

Inc row Moss st 6(2), ★ m1, moss st 4; rep from ★ to end. 46(52) sts.

Change to 4mm (US 6) needles

Beg with a k row, work 0(2) rows st st.

1st row Reading chart from right to left, k across last 19(21) sts of 1st row of Chart, k8(10)M, reading chart from left to right, k across first 19(21) sts of 1st row of Chart.

2nd row Reading chart from right to left, p across last 19(21) sts of 2nd row of Chart, p8(10)M, reading chart from left to right, p across first 19(21) sts of 2nd row of Chart.

These 2 rows set the 38(42) row patt.

Work in patt from Chart **at the same time** inc and work into st st one st at each end of the next and every foll 5th row until there are 64(72) sts.

Cont straight until 56(64) rows have been worked from top of cuff.

Cast off.

COLLAR

Join shoulder seams.

With right side facing using 4mm (US 6) needles and M slip sts from safety-pin on right front onto a needle, pick up and k21(22) sts to right shoulder, k24(26) from back neck holder, pick up and k 21(22) sts to beg of neck shaping, work across sts on safety pin. 76(80) sts.

Next row Moss st 8, k to last 8 sts, moss st 8.

Shape Collar

1st row Cast off 4 sts, moss st next 3 sts, p46(49) sts, turn.

2nd row K32(34) sts, turn.

3rd row P36(38) sts, turn.

4th row K40(42) sts, turn.

Cont in this way for a further 2 turning rows, taking an extra 4 sts, as before, on each row, turn, work to end.

Next row Cast off 4 sts, moss st next 3 sts, k to last 4 sts, moss st 4 sts.

Next row Moss st 4, p to last 4 sts, moss st 4.

Next row Moss st 4, m1, k to last 4 sts, m1, moss st 4.

Next row Moss st 4, p to last 4 sts, moss st 4.

Next row Moss st 4, k to last 4 sts, moss st 4.

Rep the last 4 rows twice more.

Moss st 5 rows across all sts.

Cast off in patt.

STRAPS (MAKE 2)

With 4mm (US 6) needles and M cast on 7 sts.

Work 8cm/3¼in in moss st.

Buttonhole row Moss st 3, yf, work 2 tog, moss st 2.

Work 2 rows.

Cont in moss st, dec one st at each end of the next 2 rows.

Next row Sl 1, k2 tog, psso and fasten off.

MAKE UP

Sew on sleeves, sewing last 6 rows to sts cast off at underarm. Join side and sleeve seams. Place straps on top of front welts and sew cast on edges to side seams. Sew on buttons.

SWEATER WITH ribbed yoke

A classic style with a textured yoke made up of ribs and simple cable twists, and a distinctive cross-over collar. This is a great project for fairly new knitters, as most of the design is worked in stocking stitch.

Materials

Debbie Bliss Cotton DK (100% cotton; 84m/91yd per 50g/1¾oz ball) DK (light worsted) weight yarn:
  9(11:13) balls of shade Leaf
Pair each of 3.75mm (US 5) and 4mm (US 6) needles
Long circular 3.75mm (US 5) needle

Measurements

To fit ages	2-3	3-4	4-5	years
Actual measurements				
Chest	72	80	88	cm
	28½	31½	34½	in
Length	35	40	45	cm
	13¾	15¾	17¾	in
Sleeve length	22	25	28	cm
	8¾	10	11	in

Tension

20 sts and 28 rows to 10cm/4in square over st st using 4mm (US 6) needles.

Abbreviations

Tw2R – k into front of 2nd st, then front of 1st st and slip both sts off the needle together.
See also page 95.

BACK

With 3.75mm (US 5) needles cast on 74(82:90) sts.
1st row K2, ★ p2, k2; rep from ★ to end.
2nd row P2, ★ k2, p2; rep from ★ to end.
Rep the last 2 rows 4(5:6) times more.
Change to 4mm (US 6) needles.
Beg with a k row, work in st st until back measures 18(21:24)/7(8¼:9½)in from cast on edge, ending with a k row.
Inc row P5(5:4), [m1, p7(8:9) sts] 9 times, m1, p6(5:5). 84(92:100) sts.
Cont in yoke patt.
1st row K3, ★ p2, Tw2R, p2, k2; rep from ★ to last 9 sts, p2, Tw2R, p2, k3.
2nd row P3, ★ k2, p2; rep from ★ to last 5 sts, k2, p3.
Rep the last 2 rows until back measures 35(40:45)cm/13¾(15¾:17¾)in from cast on edge, ending with a wrong side row.

Shape shoulders

Cast off 12(13:14) sts at beg of next 4 rows.
Leave the rem 36(40:44) sts on a holder.

FRONT

Work as given for Back until front measures 30(34:38)cm/11¾(13½:15)in from cast on edge, ending with a wrong side row.

Shape neck

Next row K31(34:37), turn and work on these sts for first side of neck.

Dec one st at neck edge on every row until 24(26:28) sts rem.

Cont straight until front measures the same as Back to shoulder, ending at side edge.

Shape shoulder

Cast off 12(13:14) sts at beg of next row.
Work 1 row.

Cast off rem 12(13:14) sts.

With right side facing, slip centre 22(24:26) sts onto a holder, rejoin yarn to rem sts, patt to end.

Complete to match first side.

SLEEVES

With 3.75mm (US 5) needles cast on 42(46:50) sts.

1st row K2, ★ p2, k2; rep from ★ to end.

2nd row P2, ★ k2, p2; rep from ★ to end.

Rep the last 2 rows 4(5:6) times more, inc 2(4:4) sts evenly across last row. 44(50:54) sts.

Change to 4mm (US 6) needles.

Work in st st, inc one st at each end of the 3rd(5th:3rd) and every foll 4th row until there are 64(70:76) sts, ending with an inc row.

Inc row P5(5:6), [m1, p18(12:9) sts] 3(5:7) times, m1, p5(5:7). 68(76:84) sts.

Cont in yoke patt.

1st row K3, ★ p2, Tw2R, p2, k2; rep from ★ to last 9 sts, p2, Tw2R, p2, k3.

2nd row P3, ★ k2, p2; rep from ★ to last 5 sts, k2, p3.

Cont in patt **at the same time** inc and work into patt one st at each end of the next and 1(2:3) foll 4th rows. 72(82:92) sts

Cont straight until sleeve measures 22(25:28)cm/8¾(10:11)in from cast on edge, ending with a wrong side row.

Cast off.

COLLAR

Join shoulder seams.

With right side facing, using 3.75mm (US 5) circular needle, slip 22(24:26) sts from centre front neck onto needle, pick up and k21(23:25) sts up right side of front neck, k across 36(40:44) sts from back neck holder, pick up and k21(23:25) sts down left side of front neck, turn and cast on 22(24:26) sts. 122(134:146) sts.

Work backwards and forwards in k2, p2, rib as folls:

Next row K2, [p2, k2] 20(22:24) times, turn.

Next row P2, [k2, p2] 10(11:12) times, turn.

Cont in rib as set.

Next 2 rows Rib to last 38(42:46) sts, turn.

Next 2 rows Rib to last 36(40:44) sts, turn.

Next 2 rows Rib to last 34(38:42) sts, turn.

Cont in this way, working 2 extra sts on every row until all sts have been worked.

Cast off loosely in rib.

MAKE UP

Sew cast on edge of collar to back of centre front sts. Sew on sleeves. Join side and sleeve seams.

SCARF WITH fair isle border

As it is worked mainly in moss stitch this scarf is reversible. Its simple Fair Isle border makes it a good project for those new to this style of knitting. For added decoration there are beads worked into the cast on and cast off rows.

Materials

Debbie Bliss Cotton DK (100% cotton; 84m/91yd per 50g/1¾oz ball) DK (light worsted) weight yarn:
  4 balls of shade White (M)
  1 ball each of shades:
  Putty (A)
  Ruby (B)
  Mint (C)
  Leaf (D)
  Pale Pink (E)
Small amount of any yellow cotton DK (light worsted) yarn (F)
Pair of 4mm (US 6) needles
14 medium-size wooden beads

Measurements

110cm x 15cm/43¼in x 6in.

Tension

21 sts and 32 rows to 10cm/4in square over moss st using 4mm (US 6) needles.

Abbreviations

See page 95.

Note

Read chart from right to left on right side rows and from left to right on wrong side rows (see page 83). When working in patt, strand yarn not in use loosely across wrong side (see page 84). For border beside patt, use a separate ball of M and the intarsia method (see page 86). Knitting with beads (see page 89).

TO MAKE

Thread seven beads onto first ball of M.
Make a slip knot and place on needle, *bring a bead up along the yarn next to the needle, cast on 5 sts; rep from * 5 times more, bring a bead up along the yarn next to the needle, cast on one st. 32 sts.
Next row [K1, p1] 7 times, k1, p2tog, * k1, p1; rep from * to last st, k1. 31 sts.
Next row K1, * p1, k1; rep from * to end.
This row sets the moss st.
Work 4 more rows in moss st.
** **Next row** Moss st 5, p21, moss st 5.
Work in patt from Chart as folls:
1st row Moss st 5, k next 21 sts from Chart, moss st 5.
This row sets the patt.
Working 5 edge sts in moss st and Chart in st st, work to end of Chart. Cont in M.
Next row Moss st 5, p21, moss st 5. ***
Next row K1, * p1, k1; rep from * to end.
This row sets the moss st.
Cont in moss st until scarf measures 105cm/41¼in from cast on edge, ending with a right side row.
Work from ** to ***.
Work 6 rows moss st across all sts, inc one st at centre of the last row. 32 sts.

Cast off row Cut the yarn approximately 1 metre (3ft) from work. Thread on seven beads. P1,* bring bead up yarn to needle and p the next st holding bead between the two sts with thumb, cast off 5 sts purlwise; rep from * ending last rep cast off one st, fasten off.

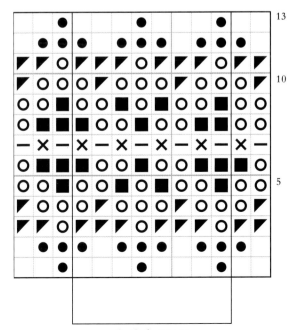

13

10

5

8 stitch repeat

Key

☐	White (M)
◥	Putty (A
✕	Ruby (B)
●	Mint (C)
■	Leaf (D)
○	Pale Pink (E)
—	Yellow (F)

BABY REEFER JACKET and hat

I love a classic double-breasted style. In this design it is achieved by simply picking up stitches from the fronts and working a double rib. Here I have teamed the jacket with the striped sweater on page 70.

Materials

Debbie Bliss Cotton DK (100% cotton; 84m/91yd per 50g/1¾oz ball) DK (light worsted) weight yarn

For the jacket:
8(9:11:12) balls of shade Ruby
Pair each of 3.75mm (US 5) and 4mm (US 6) knitting needles
6(6:8:8) buttons

For the hat:
2 balls of shade Ruby
Pair of 4mm (US 6) knitting needles

Measurements

Jacket

To fit ages	6-12	12-18	18-24	24-36 months	
Actual measurements					
Chest	64	70	76	82	cm
	25¼	27½	30	32¼	in
Length to shoulder	30	35	39	43	cm
	11¾	13¾	15½	17	in
Sleeve length	18	20	23	26	cm
(cuff turned back)	7	8	9	10¼	in

Hat

To fit ages	6-18	18-36	months

Tension

20 sts and 28 rows to 10cm/4in square over st st using 4mm (US 6) needles.

Abbreviations

See page 95.

JACKET

BACK

With 3.75mm (US 5) needles cast on 66(70:78:82) sts.

1st row K2, ★ p2, k2; rep from ★ to end.

2nd row P2, ★ k2, p2; rep from ★ to end

Rep the last 2 rows for 7cm/2¾in, ending with a 2nd row and inc 0(2:0:2) sts evenly across last row. 66(72:78:84) sts.

Change to 4mm (US 6) needles.

Beg with a k row cont in st st until back measures 30(35:39:43)cm/11¾(13¾:15½:17)in from cast on edge, ending with a p row.

Shape shoulders

Cast off 11(12:13:14) sts at beg of next 2 rows and 12(13:14:14) sts at beg of foll 2 rows.

Cast off rem 20(22:24:28) sts on a spare needle.

LEFT FRONT

With 3.75mm (US 5) needles cast on 23(23:27:27) sts.

1st row K2, ★ p2, k2; rep from ★ to last 5 sts, p2, k3.

2nd row P3, ★ k2, p2; rep from ★ to end.

Rep the last 2 rows for 7cm/2¾in, ending with a 2nd row and inc 0(2:0:1) sts evenly across last row. 23(25:27:28) sts.

Change to 4mm (US 6) needles.

Beg with a k row cont in st st until front measures 30(35:39:43)cm/11¾(13¾:15½:17)in from cast on edge, ending with a p row.

Shape shoulder

Cast off 11(12:13:14) sts at beg of next row.

Work 1 row.

Cast off rem 12(13:14:14) sts.

RIGHT FRONT

With 3.75mm (US 5) needles cast on
23(23:27:27) sts.

1st row K3, ★ p2, k2; rep from ★ to end.

2nd row P2, ★ k2, p2; rep from ★ to last 5 sts,
k2, p3.

Rep the last 2 rows for 7cm/2¾in, ending
with a 2nd row and inc 0(2:0:1) sts evenly
across last row. 23(25:27:28) sts.

Change to 4mm (US 6) needles.

Beg with a k row cont in st st until front
measures 30(35:39:43)cm/11¾(13¾:15½:17)in
from cast on edge, ending with a k row.

Shape shoulder

Cast off 11(12:13:14) sts at beg of next row.

Work 1 row.

Cast off rem 12(13:14:14) sts.

SLEEVES

With 4mm (US 6) needles cast on
38(42:42:46) sts.

1st row K2, ★ p2, k2; rep from ★ to end.

2nd row P2, ★ k2, p2; rep from ★ to end

Rep the last 2 rows for 5cm/2in, ending with
a 2nd row.

Change to 3.75mm (US 5) needles.

Work a further 5cm/2in in rib, ending with a
2nd row, inc 6 sts evenly across last row.
44(48:48:52) sts.

Change to 4mm (US 6) needles.

Beg with a k row, work in st st, inc one st at
each end of the 3rd and every foll 4th row
until there are 58(64:68:74) sts.

Cont straight until sleeve measures
23(25:28:31)cm/9(10:11:12¼)in from cast on
edge, ending with a p row.

Cast off.

FRONTBANDS AND COLLAR

Join shoulder seams.

With 3.75mm (US 5) needles and right side facing, pick up
and k71(82:93:101) sts up right front to shoulder seam,
20(22:24:28) sts from back neck, 71(82:93:101) sts down left
front. 162(186:210:230) sts.

1st row P2, ★ k2, p2; rep from ★ to end.

This row sets the rib.

Next 2 rows Rib to last 65(75:86:94) sts, turn.

Next 2 rows Rib to last 59(69:79:87) sts, turn.

Next 2 rows Rib to last 53(63:72:80) sts, turn.

Next 2 rows Rib to last 47(57:65:73) sts, turn.

Next row Rib to end.

Rib 3 more rows.

Buttonhole row Rib 4, [work 2 tog, yf, rib 14(16:14:16)]
2(2:3:3) times, work 2 tog, yf, rib to end.

Rib 13(15:17:19) more rows.

Divide for collar shaping

Next row Rib 59(68:77:84), turn.

Rib 3 rows.

Rep the buttonhole row.

Rib 5 more rows.

Cast off in rib.

With 3.75mm (US 5) needles and right side facing, rejoin
yarn to rem sts, rib 44(50:56:62) sts, turn.

Rib 9 rows.

Cast off in rib.
With 3.75mm (US 5) needles and right side facing, rejoin yarn to rem sts, rib to end.
Rib 9 rows.
Cast off in rib.

MAKE UP

With centre of sleeves to shoulder seam, sew on sleeves. Join side and sleeve seams.
Sew on buttons.

HAT
TO MAKE

With 4mm (US 6) needles cast on 82(90) sts.
1st rib row K2, ★ p2, k2; rep from ★ to end.
2nd rib row P2, ★ k2, p2; rep from ★ to end.
Rep the last 2 rows until hat measures 16(18)cm/6¼(7)in from cast on edge, ending with a 2nd rib row.

Shape top

1st row K2, ★p2 tog, k2; rep from ★ to end. 62(68)sts.
2nd row P2, ★ k1, p2; rep from ★ to end.
3rd row K2, ★ p1, k2; rep from ★ to end.
4th row P2, ★ k1, p2; rep from ★ to end.
5th row K2 tog, ★p1, k2 tog; rep from ★ to end. 41(45) sts.
6th row P1, ★ k1, p1; rep from ★ to end.
7th row K1, ★ p3 tog, k1; rep from ★ to end. 21(23) sts.
8th row P1, ★ p2 tog; rep from ★ to end.
Break off yarn, thread end through rem sts, pull up and secure.
Join seam. Make a small pom-pom and sew to crown.

GUERNSEY dress

This pretty dress for a baby is inspired by traditional fisherman or Guernsey sweaters. The patterned yoke is a patchwork of neat cables, moss-stitch hearts, and lace and bobbles. There are also matching bootees, see page 38, and a throw, see page 66.

Materials

Debbie Bliss Baby Cashmerino (55% wool, 33% acrylic, 12% cashmere; 125m/137yd per 50g/1¾oz ball) light DK (sport) weight yarn:
  5(6:8) 50g balls of shade Lilac
Pair each of 3mm (US 2) and 3.25mm (US 3) knitting needles
Cable needle
1st size only 3 buttons

Measurements

To fit ages	6-12	12-18	24-36	months.
Actual measurements				
Chest	56	64	70	cm
	22	25¼	27½	in
Length to shoulder	36	40	45	cm
	14¼	15¾	17¾in	in
Sleeve length	18	20	22	cm
	7	8	8¾	in

Tension

25 sts and 34 rows to 10cm/4in square over st st using 3.25mm (US 3) needles.

Abbreviations

Mb – work k1, p1, k1, p1, k1, into next st, turn, p5, turn, pass 2nd, 3rd, 4th and 5th st over first and off the needle, then pass st back onto right hand needle.
C4F – slip next 2 sts onto cable needle and hold at front of work, k2, then k2 from cable needle.
Also see pages 88 and 95.

PANEL A

(worked over 15 sts)
1st row K to end.
2nd row P to end.
3rd row K7, p1, k7.
4th row P6, k1, p1, k1, p6.
5th row K5, p1, [k1, p1] twice, k5.
6th row P4, k1, [p1, k1] 3 times, p4.
7th row K3, p1, [k1, p1] 4 times, k3.
8th row P2, k1, [p1, k1] 5 times, p2.
9th row K1, [p1, k1] 7 times.
10th row As 8th row.
11th row As 9th row.
12th row As 8th row.
13th row [K1, p1] 3 times, k3, [p1, k1] 3 times.
14th row P2, k1, p1, k1, p5, k1, p1, k1, p2.
15th row K to end.
16th row P to end.

17th row K to end.
18th row P to end.
These 18 rows form the patt panel.

PANEL B
(worked over 15 sts)
1st row K to end.
2nd and alt rows P to end.
3rd row K to end.
5th row K6, k2 tog, yf, k7.
7th row K5, k2 tog, yf, k1, yf, skpo, k5.
9th row K4, k2 tog, yf, k3, yf, skpo, k4.
11th row K3, k2 tog, yf, k2, Mb, k2, yf, skpo, k3.
13th row K2, k2 tog, yf, k7, yf, skpo, k2.
15th row K1, k2 tog, yf, k2, Mb, k3, Mb, k2, yf, skpo, k1.
17th row K to end.
18th row P to end.
These 18 rows form the patt panel.

The Guernsey Dress and matching Lace and Bobble Bootees.

PANEL C
(worked over 15 sts)
1st row K to end.
2nd and alt rows P to end.
3rd row K6, Mb, k2, [k2 tog, yf] twice, k2.
5th row K8, [k2 tog, yf] twice, k3.
7th row K7, [k2 tog, yf] twice, k4.
9th row K3, Mb, k2, [k2 tog, yf] twice, k5.
11th row K7, [yf, skpo] twice, k4.
13th row K8, [yf, skpo] twice, k3.
15th row K6, Mb, k2, [yf, skpo] twice, k2.
17th row K to end.
18th row P to end.
These 18 rows form the patt panel.

PANEL D
(worked over 15 sts)
1st row K to end.
2nd and alt rows P to end.

3rd row K2, [yf, skpo] twice, k2, Mb, k6.

5th row K3, [yf, skpo] twice, k8.

7th row K4, [yf, skpo] twice, k7.

9th row K5, [yf, skpo] twice, k2, Mb, k3.

11th row K4, [k2 tog, yf] twice, k7.

13th row K3, [k2 tog, yf] twice, k8.

15th row K2, [k2 tog, yf] twice, k2, Mb, k6.

17th row K to end.

18th row P to end.

These 18 rows form the patt panel.

BACK

With 3mm (US 2) needles cast on 105(117:127) sts.

1st row (right side) K1, *p1, k1; rep from * to end.

This row forms the moss st.

Work a further 5 rows.

Change to 3.25mm (US 3) needles.

Beg with a k row cont in st st until back measures 14(17:21)cm/5½(6¾:8¼)in from cast on edge, ending with a k row.

Dec row P2(5:7), [p2 tog, p1] 33(35:37) times, p2 tog, p2(5:7). 71(81:89) sts.

Cont in patt as folls:

1st size only

1st row * K1, [p1, k1] 10 times, C4F; rep from * once more, k1, [p1, k1] 10 times.

2nd row * K1, [p1, k1] 10 times, p4; rep from * once more, k1, [p1, k1] 10 times.

3rd row * K1, [p1, k1] 10 times, k4; rep from * once more, k1, [p1, k1] 10 times.

4th row * K1, [p1, k1] 10 times, p4; rep from * once more, k1, [p1, k1] 10 times.

These 4 rows form cable and moss st patt panel.

5th row Moss st 3, work 1st row of patt panel A, patt 10, work 1st row of patt panel B, patt 10, work 1st row of patt panel A, moss st 3.

6th row Moss st 3, work 2nd row of patt panel A, patt 10, work 2nd row of patt panel B, patt 10, work 2nd row of patt panel A, moss st 3.

7th to 22nd rows Rep 5th and 6th rows eight times, working 3rd to 18th rows of patt panels.

23rd row * K1, [p1, k1] 10 times, k4; rep from * once more, k1, [p1, k1] 10 times.

24th row * K1, [p1, k1] 10 times, p4; rep from * once more, k1, [p1, k1] 10 times.

25th row * K1, [p1, k1] 10 times, C4F; rep from * once more, k1, [p1, k1] 10 times.

26th row * K1, [p1, k1] 10 times, p4; rep from * once more, k1, [p1, k1] 10 times.

27th row Moss st 3, work 1st row of patt panel C, patt 10, work 1st row of patt panel A, patt 10, work 1st row of patt panel D, moss st 3.

28th row Moss st 3, work 2nd row of patt panel D, patt 10, work 2nd row of patt panel A, patt 10, work 2nd row of patt panel C, moss st 3.

29th to 44th rows Rep 7th and 8th rows eight times, working 3rd to 18th rows of patt panels.

45th row to 66th rows As 1st to 22nd rows, working p2 tog over each cable on last row. 69 sts.

2nd size only

1st row K1, C4F, * k1, [p1, k1] 10 times, C4F; rep from * once more, [k1, p1] 10 times, k1, C4F, k1.

2nd row K1, p4, * k1, [p1, k1] 10 times, p4; rep from * once more, k1, [p1, k1] 10 times, p4, k1.

3rd row K5, * k1, [p1, k1] 10 times, k4; rep from * once more, [k1, p1] 10 times, k6.

4th row K1, p4, * k1, [p1, k1] 10 times, p4; rep from * once more, k1, [p1, k1] 10 times, p4, k1.

These 4 rows form cable and moss st patt panel.

5th row Patt 8, work 1st row of patt panel A, patt 10, work 1st row of patt panel B, patt 10, work 1st row of patt panel A, patt 8.

6th row Patt 8, work 2nd row of patt panel A, patt 10, work 2nd row of patt panel B, patt 10, work 2nd row of patt panel A, patt 8.

7th to 22nd rows Rep 5th and 6th rows eight times, working 3rd to 18th rows of patt panels.

23rd row K5, * k1, [p1, k1] 10 times, k4; rep from * once more, [k1, p1] 10 times, k6.

24th row K1, p4, * k1, [p1, k1] 10 times, p4; rep from * once more, k1, [p1, k1] 10 times, p4, k1.

25th row K1, C4F, * k1, [p1, k1] 10 times, C4F; rep from * once more, [k1, p1] 10 times, k1, C4F, k1.

26th row K1, p4, * k1, [p1, k1] 10 times, p4; rep from * once more, k1, [p1, k1] 10 times, p4, k1.

27th row Patt 8, work 1st row of patt panel C, patt 10, work 1st row of patt panel A, patt 10, work 1st row of patt panel D, patt 8.

28th row Patt 8, work 2nd row of patt panel D, patt 10, work 2nd row of patt panel A, patt 10, work 2nd row of patt panel C, patt 8.

29th to 44th rows Rep 7th and 8th rows eight times, working 3rd to 18th rows of patt panel.

45th row to 66th rows As 1st to 22nd rows, working p2 tog over each cable on last row. 77 sts.

3rd size only

1st row P1, k1, C4F, ★ k1, [p1, k1] 11 times, C4F; rep from ★ once more, [k1, p1] 11 times, k1, C4F, k1, p1.

2nd row P1, k1, p4, ★ k1, [p1, k1] 11 times, p4; rep from ★ once more, k1, [p1, k1] 11 times, p4, k1, p1.

3rd row P1, k5, ★ k1, [p1, k1] 11 times, k4; rep from ★ once more, [k1, p1] 11 times, k6, p1.

4th row P1, k1, p4, ★ k1, [p1, k1] 11 times, p4; rep from ★ once more, k1, [p1, k1] 11 times, p4, k1, p1.

These 4 rows form cable and moss st patt panel.

5th row Patt 10, work 1st row of patt panel A, patt 12, work 1st row of patt panel B, patt 12, work 1st row of patt panel A, patt 10.

6th row Patt 10, work 2nd row of patt panel A, patt 12, work 2nd row of patt panel B, patt 12, work 2nd row of patt panel A, patt 10.

7th to 22nd rows Rep 5th and 6th rows eight times, working 3rd to 18th rows of patt panels.

23rd row P1, k5, ★ k1, [p1, k1] 11 times, k4; rep from ★ once more, [k1, p1] 11 times, k6, p1.

24th row P1, k1, p4, ★ k1, [p1, k1] 11 times, p4; rep from ★ once more, k1, [p1, k1] 11 times, p4, k1, p1.

25th row P1, k1, C4F, ★ k1, [p1, k1] 11 times, C4F; rep from ★ once more, [k1, p1] 11 times, k1, C4F, k1, p1.

26th row P1, k1, p4, ★ k1, [p1, k1] 11 times, p4; rep from ★ once more, k1, [p1, k1] 11 times, p4, k1, p1.

27th row Patt 10, work 1st row of patt panel C, patt 12, work 1st row of patt panel A, patt 12, work 1st row of patt panel D, patt 10.

28th row Patt 10, work 2nd row of patt panel D, patt 12, work 2nd row of patt panel A, patt 12, work 2nd row of patt panel C, patt 10.

29th to 44th rows Rep 7th and 8th rows eight times, working rows 3rd to 18th rows of patt panels.

45th row to 66th rows As 1st to 22nd rows, working p2 tog over each cable on last row. 85 sts.

All sizes

Work 17(21:25) rows moss st across all sts.

Shape shoulders

1st size only

Buttonband

Next row Moss st 20, turn.

Work 2 rows on these sts.

Cast off.

With wrong side facing, rejoin yarn to rem sts, patt to end.

Next row Cast off 20 sts, patt to end.

Leave rem sts on a holder.

2nd and 3rd size only

Cast off (23:26) sts at beg of next 2 rows.

Leave rem (31:33) sts on a holder.

FRONT

Work as given for Back until 66 rows have been worked in patt.

All sizes

Work 4 rows moss st across all sts.

Shape neck

Next row Patt 26(29:32) sts, turn and work on these sts for first side of front neck.

Dec one st at neck edge on next 6 rows. 20(23:26) sts.

Work 7(11:15) rows straight.

1st size only

Buttonhole row Moss st 4, yon, work 2 tog, moss st 8, yon, work 2 tog, moss st 4.

Work 2 rows moss st.

3rd row [K1, p1] 1(2:3) times, C4F, ★ p1, [k1, p1] 3 times, C4F; rep from ★ twice more, [p1, k1] 1(2:3) times.

4th row K1, [p1, k1] 0(1:2) times, p6, ★ [k1, p1] twice, k1, p6; rep from ★ twice more, k1, [p1, k1] 0(1:2) times.

These 4 rows **set** the position of cable and moss st patt panels.

Cont in patt, inc one st at each end of the next and every foll 4th row until there are 67(73:83) sts, working inc sts into moss st and cable patt.

Cont straight until sleeve measures 18(20:22)cm/7(8:8¾)in from cast on edge, ending with a wrong side row.

Cast off, working 2 sts tog over cables.

NECKBAND

Join right shoulder seam.

With right side facing using 3mm (US 2) needles, pick up and k14(12:14) sts down left front neck, k17(19:21) sts from centre front holder, pick up and k9(11:13) sts up right front neck, k29(31:33) sts from centre back holder, then for 1st size only pick up and k4 sts along buttonband.

73(73:81) sts.

Next row K1, ★ p1, k1; rep from ★ to end. This row forms the moss st.

1st size only

Next row Patt 2, yon, work 2 tog, patt to end.

All sizes

Moss st 3(4:6) rows.

Cast off.

MAKE UP

1st size only

Lap buttonhole band over buttonband and catch side edges together. Sew on buttons.

2nd and 3rd sizes only

Join shoulder and neckband seam.

All sizes

Sew on sleeves. Join side and sleeve seams.

All sizes

Shape shoulder

Cast off.

With right side facing, slip centre 17(19:21) sts on a holder, rejoin yarn to rem sts, patt to end.

Dec one st at neck edge on next 6 rows. 20(23:26) sts.

Work 6(10:14) rows straight.

Cast off.

SLEEVES

With 3mm (US 2) needles cast on 37(41:45) sts.

1st row (right side) K1, ★p1, k1; rep from ★ to end. This row forms the moss st.

Work a further 7 rows.

Change to 3.25mm (US 3) needles.

Inc row Moss st 3(5:7), [m1, moss st 10] 3 times, m1, moss st 4(6:8). 41(45:49) sts.

Cont in patt as folls:

1st row [K1, p1] 1(2:3) times, k4, ★ p1, [k1, p1] 3 times, k4; rep from ★ twice more, [p1, k1] 1(2:3) times.

2nd row K1, [p1, k1] 0(1:2) times, p6, ★ [k1, p1] twice, k1, p6; rep from ★ twice more, k1, [p1, k1] 0(1:2) times.

LACE AND BOBBLE bootees

These bootees are designed to match the Guernsey Dress (page 32) and the Lace and Bobble Baby Throw (page 66).

Materials
Debbie Bliss Baby Cashmerino (55% wool, 33% acrylic, 12% cashmere; 125m/137yd per 50g/1¾oz ball) light DK (sport) weight yarn:
   1 ball of shade Lilac
Pair of 2.75mm (US 2) knitting needles
2 buttons

Measurements
To fit   6 months

Tension
25 sts and 34 rows to 10cm/4in square over st st using 3.25mm (US 3) needles.

Abbreviations
Mb – work k1, p1, k1, p1, k1, into next st, turn, p5, turn, pass 2nd, 3rd, 4th and 5th st over first and off the needle, then pass st back onto right hand needle.
Also see page 95.

RIGHT SHOE
With 2.75mm (US 2) needles cast on 34 sts.
K 1 row.
1st row K1, yf, k15, [yf, k1] twice, yf, k15, yf, k1.
2nd row and 4 foll alt rows K to end, working k1 tbl into yf of previous row.
3rd row K2, yf, k15, yf, k2, yf, k3, yf, k15, yf, k2.
5th row K3, yf, k15, [yf, k4] twice, yf, k15, yf, k3.
7th row K4, yf, k15, yf, k5, yf, k6, yf, k15, yf, k4.
9th row K5, yf, k15, [yf, k7] twice, yf, k15, yf, k5.
11th row K7, yf, [k9, yf] 5 times, k7. 65 sts.
12th row K to end, working k1 tbl into yf of previous row.
Next row K1, ★ p1, k1; rep from ★ to end.
Rep the last row 11 times more.

Shape instep
1st row Patt 25, k14, skpo, turn.
2nd row Sl 1, p13, p2 tog, turn.
3rd row Sl 1, k5, k2 tog, yf, k6, skpo, turn.
4th row Sl 1, p13, p2 tog, turn.
5th row Sl 1, k4, k2 tog, yf, k1, yf, skpo, k4, skpo, turn.
6th row Sl 1, p13, p2 tog, turn.
7th row Sl 1, k3, k2 tog, yf, k3, yf, skpo, k3, skpo, turn.
8th row Sl 1, p13, p2 tog, turn.
9th row Sl 1, k2, k2 tog, yf, k2, Mb, k2, yf, skpo, k2, skpo, turn.
10th row Sl 1, p13, p2 tog, turn.
11th row Sl 1, k1, k2 tog, yf, k7, yf, skpo, k1, skpo, turn.

12th row Sl 1, p13, p2 tog, turn.
13th row Sl 1, k2 tog, yf, k2, Mb, k3, Mb, k2, yf, [skpo] twice, turn.
14th row Sl 1, p13, p2 tog, turn.
15th row Sl 1, k14, patt to end.
Cast off, dec one st at each corner.
Join sole and back seam.
With 2.75mm (US 2) needles, right side facing and beginning and ending within 8 sts of back seam, pick up and k15 sts evenly along heel.
Next row P1, ★ k1, p1; rep from ★ to end. ★★
Next row Cast on 3 sts, k1, p1, k1, patt to end, turn and cast on 19 sts.
Next row K1, ★ p1, k1; rep from ★ to end.
Buttonhole row Patt 33, yf, k2 tog, p1, k1.
Patt 2 rows.
Cast off.

LEFT SHOE
Work as given for Right Shoe to ★★.
Next row Cast on 19 sts, k1, [p1, k1] 9 times, turn and cast on 3 sts.
Next row K1, ★ p1, k1; rep from ★ to end.
Buttonhole row K1, p1, k2 tog, yf, patt to end.
Patt 2 rows.
Cast off.

TUNIC WITH contrast edging

An ideal design for inexperienced knitters who want to introduce some colour into a project, without embarking on complicated Fair Isle or intarsia. The simple stocking stitch tunic is enlivened with contrast borders and pocket linings.

Materials
Debbie Bliss Cotton DK (100% cotton; 84m/91yd per 50g/1¾oz ball) DK (light worsted) weight yarn:
6(7:9) balls of shade Duck Egg (M)
1 ball each of shades:
Heather (A)
Ruby (B)
Mint (C)
Pair each of 3.75mm (US 5) and 4mm (US 6) knitting needles

Measurements

To fit ages	1	2	3	years.
Actual measurements				
Chest	64	72	80	cm
	25¼	28½	31½	in
Length to shoulder	36	40	46	cm
	14¼	15¾	18	in
Sleeve length	19	22	25	cm
	7½	8¾	10	in

Tension
20 sts and 28 rows to 10cm/4in square over st st using 4mm (US 6) needles.

Abbreviations
See page 95.

BACK
With 3.75mm (US 5) needles and A cast on 66(74:82) sts.
1st row K2, ★ p2, k2; rep from ★ to end.
2nd row P to end.
Rep the last 2 rows 5(6:7) times more.
Change to 4mm (US 6) needles and yarn M.
Beg with a k row, cont in st st until back measures 20(23:26)cm/8(9:10¼)in from cast on edge, ending with a p row.

Shape armholes
Cast off 5 sts at beg of next 2 rows.
56(64:72) sts.
Cont in st st until back measures 34(38:44)cm/13½(15:17¼)in from cast on edge, ending with a p row.

Shape Neck
Next row K20(23:26) turn and work on these sts for first side of back neck.
Dec one st at neck edge on next 4 rows.
16(19:22) sts
Work 1 row straight.

Shape shoulder
Cast off 8(9:11) sts at beg of next row.
Work 1 row.
Cast off rem 8(10:11) sts.
With right side facing, slip centre 16(18:20) sts onto a holder, join on yarn, k to end.
Complete to match first side of neck.

Shape armholes

Cast off 5 sts at beg of next 2 rows.
56(64:72) sts.
Cont in st st until front measures
32(35:40)cm/12½(13¾:15¾)in from
cast on edge, ending with a p row.

Shape Neck

Next row K22(25:28) turn and
work on these sts for first side of
front neck.
Dec one st at neck edge on every
row until 16(19:22) sts rem.
Work straight until front measures
same as Back to shoulder, ending at
armhole edge.

Shape shoulder

Cast off 8(9:11) sts at beg of
next row.
Work 1 row.
Cast off rem 8(10:11) sts.
With right side facing, slip centre
12(14:16) sts onto a holder, join on
yarn, k to end. Complete to match
first side of neck.

POCKET LININGS (MAKE 2)

With 4mm (US 6) needles and yarn B cast on
18(22:22) sts.
Beg with a k row work 19(21:23) rows in st
st, ending with a k row.
Leave these sts on a spare needle.

FRONT

With 3.75mm (US 5) needles and yarn A cast
on 66(74:82) sts.
1st row K2, ★ p2, k2; rep from ★ to end.
2nd row P to end.
Rep the last 2 rows 5(6:7) times more.
Change to 4mm (US 6) needles and yarn M.
Beg with a k row, work 18(20:22) rows in st
st, ending with a p row.

Place pocket

Next row K7(7:9) sts, k next 18(22:22) sts and leave
these sts on a holder, k16(16:20), k next 18(22:22)
sts and leave these sts on a holder, k last 7(7:9) sts.
Next row P7(7:9) sts, p across 18(22:22) sts of
one pocket lining, p16(16:20), p across 18(22:22)
sts of second pocket lining, p7(7:9).
Beg with a k row, cont in st st until front
measures 20(23:26)cm/8(9:10¼)in from cast
on edge, ending with a p row.

SLEEVES

With 3.75mm (US 5) needles and yarn C, cast on
30(34:38) sts.
Work 9(11:13) rows rib as given for back.
Inc row P2(4:6), m1, [p5, m1] 5 times, p3(5:7).
36(40:44) sts.
Change to 4mm (US 6) needles and yarn M.
Beg with a k row, cont in st st, inc one st at each end of
every 3rd row until there are 64(70:78) sts.
Work straight until sleeve measures 19(22:25)cm/7½
(8¾:10)in from cast on edge, ending with a p row.
Work a further 8 rows.
Cast off.

NECKBAND

Join right shoulder seam.
With right side facing, 3.75mm (US 5) needles and yarn B,
pick up and k14 sts down left side of front neck, k across
12(14:16) sts from front neck holder, pick up and k14 sts up
right side of front neck, 7 sts from right back neck,
k16(18:20) across sts from back neck holder, pick up and k 7
sts from left back neck. 70(74:78) sts.
1st row P2. ★ k2, p2; rep from ★ to end.
2nd row K to end.
Rep the last 2 rows 3 times more.

Change to 4mm (US 6) needles.
1st row K to end.
2nd row P2. ★ k2, p2; rep from ★ to end.
Rep the last 2 rows 3 times more and the 1st row
again.
Cast off in rib.
POCKET TOPS
With right side facing, 3.75mm (US 5) needles and
yarn C, k across 18(22:22) sts of pocket front.
1st row P2. ★ k2, p2; rep from ★ to end.
2nd row K to end.
3rd row P2. ★ k2, p2; rep from ★ to end.
Cast off.

TO MAKE UP
Join left shoulder and neckband seam, reversing final 9
rows to fold over. Sew on sleeves, sew last 8 rows to
sts cast off at under arm. Join side and sleeve seams.
Sew down pocket linings and pocket tops.

ZIPPED JACKET with hood

A good, all-year-round jacket with a cabled yoke and hood. There are no increasings before the yoke, giving it the slightly A-line shape that I love on small children, while the zip gives it a sporty edge.

Materials
Debbie Bliss Cotton DK (100% cotton; 84m/91yd per 50g/1¾oz ball) DK (light worsted) weight yarn:
 11(12:13) balls of shade French Navy
Pair each of 3.75mm (US 5) and 4mm (US 6) knitting needles
Cable needle
35(40:45)cm/ 14(16:18)in open-ended zipper

Measurements

To fit ages	2-3	4-5	6-7	years
Actual measurements				
Chest	80	94	108	cm
	31½	37	42½	in
Length to shoulder	40	45	50	cm
	15¾	17¾	19¾	in
Sleeve length	25	27	30	cm
	10	10½	11¾	in

Tension
20 sts and 28 rows to 10cm/4in square over st st using 4mm (US 6) needles.
21 sts and 30 rows to 10cm/4in square over cable patt using 4mm (US 6) needles.

Abbreviations
C4F – slip next 2 sts onto cable needle and leave at front, k2, then k2 from cable needle.
C4B – slip next 2 sts onto cable needle and leave at back, k2, then k2 from cable needle.
See also pages 88 and 95.

BACK
With 3.75mm (US 5) needles cast on 84(99:114) sts.
K 2 rows.
Change to 4mm (US 6) needles.
Beg with a k row, cont in st st until back measures 20(23:26)cm/8(9:10¼)in, ending with a p row.
Cont in yoke patt:
Next row ★[P1, k1] 4 times, p1, k2, C4F; rep from ★ to last 9 sts, [p1, k1] 4 times, p1.
Next row P1, ★ k1, p5, k1, p8; rep from ★ to last 8 sts, k1, p5, k1, p1.
Next row ★[P1, k1] 4 times, p1, C4B, k2; rep from ★ to last 9 sts, [p1, k1] 4 times, p1.
Next row P1, ★ k1, p5, k1, p8; rep from ★ to last 8 sts, k1, p5, k1, p1.
Rep last 4 rows until back measures 40(45:50)cm/15¾(17¾:19¾)in, ending with a wrong side row.

Shape shoulders
Cast off 12(14:16) sts at the beg of the next 4 rows.
Cast off rem 36(43:50) sts.

LEFT FRONT
With 3.75mm (US 5) needles cast on 40(49:55) sts.
1st row K to last 4 sts, [p1, k1] twice.
2nd row [K1, p1] twice, k to end.
Change to 4mm (US 6) needles.
3rd row K to last 4 sts, [p1, k1] twice.
4th row K1, p1, k1, p to end.
Keeping 4 edge sts in moss st and the rem sts

in st st work 8(10:12) rows, ending with a wrong side row.

Shape pocket

Next row K12(14:16) sts, turn and place rem sts on a holder, cast on 24(26:28) sts. 36(40:44) sts.

Beg with a p row work 29(31:33) rows st st. Leave these sts on a spare needle.

With right side facing, rejoin yarn to sts at centre front.

Next row K to last 4 sts, [p1, k1] twice.

Next row K1, p1, k1, p to last 2 sts, k2.

Rep the last 2 rows 14(15:16) times more, ending with a wrong side row.

Return to first set of sts on holder.

K the first 12(14:16) sts, place the pocket lining behind sts of front, then [k next st on front tog with next st from pocket lining] 24(26:28) times, patt to end.

Keeping the edge 4 sts in moss st and rem sts in st st, work until front measures 20(23:26)cm/8(9:10¼)in, ending with a wrong side row.

Next row ★P1, [k1, p1] 4 times, k2, C4F; rep from ★ 1(2:2) times, p1, [k1, p1] 4(1:4) times, k1.

Next row K1, p1, [k1, p8] 0(1:0) times, [k1, p5, k1, p8] 2(2:3) times, k1, p5, k1, p1.

Next row ★P1, [k1, p1] 4 times, C4B, k2; rep from ★ 1(2:2) times, p1, [k1, p1] 4(1:4) times, k1.

Next row K1, p1, [k1, p8] 0 (1, 0) times [k1, p5, k1, p8] 2(2:3) times, k1, p5, k1, p1.

Rep the last 4 rows until left front measures 35(40:45)cm/13¾(15¾:17¾)in, ending with a right side row.

Shape neck

Next row Cast off 7(9:11) sts, work to end.

Dec one st at neck edge on every row until 24(28:32) sts rem.

Work straight until front matches Back to shoulder shaping, ending at side edge.

Shape shoulder

Cast off 12(14:16) sts at the beg of the next row.

Work 1 row.

Cast off rem 12(14:16) sts

RIGHT FRONT

Using 3.75mm (US 5) needles cast on 40(49:55) sts.

1st row P1, k1, p1, k to end

2nd row K to last 3 sts p1, k1, p1.

Change to 4mm (US 6) needles.

3rd row P1, k1, p1, k to end.

4th row P to last 4 sts, [k1, p1] twice.

Keeping 4 edge sts in moss st and the rem sts in st st work 8(10:12) rows, ending with a wrong side row.

Shape pocket

Next row Patt 28(35:39), turn and place rem sts on a spare needle.

Next row P to last 4 sts, [k1, p1] twice.

Work a further 28(30:32) rows as set.

Leave these sts on a spare needle.

Return to first set of sts on spare needle.

Cast on 24(26:28) sts, k these sts, then with right side facing, k across sts on spare needle.

Beg with a p row, work 29(31:33) rows in st st.

With right side facing, rejoin yarn to sts at centre front.

Patt the first 4(9:11) sts, place the pocket lining behind sts of front, then [k next st on front tog with next st from pocket lining] 24(26:28) times, k to end.

Keeping the edge 4 sts in moss st and rem sts in st st, work until front measures 20(23:26)cm/8(9:10¼)in, ending with a wrong side row.

Next row [K1, p1] 5(2:5) times, ★ k2, C4F, [p1, k1] 4 times, p1; rep from ★1(2:2) times.

Next row P1, k1, p5, ★ k1, p8, k1, p5; rep from ★ 1(1:2) times, k1, p1(8:1), k1, p0(1:0), k0(1:0).

Next row [K1, p1] 5(2:5) times, ★ C4B, k2, [p1, k1] 4 times, p1; rep from ★1(2:2) times.

Next row P1, k1, p5, ★ k1, p8, k1, p5; rep from ★ 1(1:2) times, k1, p1(8:1), k1, p0(1:0), k0(1:0).

Rep the last 4 rows until right front measures 35(40:45cm)/13¾(15¾:17¾)in, ending with a wrong side row.

Shape neck

Next row Cast off 7(9:11) sts, work to end.

Dec one st at neck edge on every row until 24(28:32) sts rem.

Work straight until front matches Back to shoulder shaping, ending at side edge.

Shape shoulder

Cast off 12(14:16) sts at the beg of the next row.

Work 1 row.

Cast off rem 12(14:16) sts

SLEEVES

With 3.75mm (US 5) needles cast on 44(52:60) sts.

K 2 rows.

Change to 4mm (US 6) needles.

Cont in patt.

1st row K1(1:3), p1, [k1, p1] 1(3:4) times, ★ k2, C4F, p1, [k1, p1] 4 times; rep from ★ once more, k2, C4F, [p1, k1] 1(3:4) times, p1, k1(1:3).

2nd row P0(0:4), k0(1:1), p2(5:5), ★ k1, p8, k1, p5; rep from ★ once more, k1, p8, k1, p2(5:5), k0(1:1), p0(0:4).

3rd row K1(1:3), p1, [k1, p1] 1(3:4) times, ★ C4B, k2, p1, [k1, p1] 4 times; rep from ★ once more, C4B, k2, [p1, k1] 1(3:4) times, p1, k1(1:3).

4th row P0(0:4), k0(1:1), p2(5:5), ★ k1, p8, k1, p5; rep from ★ once more, k1, p8, k1, p2(5:5), k0(1:1), p0(0:4).

These 4 rows set the patt.

Cont in patt **at the same time** inc one st at each end of next and every foll 4th row until there are 82(92:102) sts.

Cont straight until sleeve measures 25(27:30)cm/10(10½:11¾)in from cast on edge ending with a wrong side row.

Cast off.

HOOD

Join shoulder seams.

With 4mm (US 6) needles and right side facing, pick up and k22(28:34) sts along left front neck, 37(43:51) sts across back neck, 22(28:34) sts along right front neck. 81(99:119) sts.

Next row: K2, p1, [k1, p1] to last 2 sts, k2.

Rep the last row until hood measures 24(27:29)cm/9½(10½:11½)in dec one st at centre of last row.

Next row Patt 40(49:59) sts, with right sides tog, fold hood in half and cast off the sts of the hood tog by knitting into the first st on one needle and the first st on the other needle, k tog until 2 sts are on the right hand needle, cast off one st, cont until all sts are cast off.

MAKE UP

Sew on sleeves, placing centre of sleeves to shoulder seams. Join side and sleeve seams. Sew in zip. Sew down pocket linings.

CABLE SWEATER with pocket

This classic long-line aran sweater contrasts cables and bobbles with a deep welt in a subtle chevron pattern. The pocket, borders and cuffs are edged with light blue. This design is for the more experienced knitter.

Materials

Debbie Bliss Cotton DK (100% cotton; 84m/91yd per 50g/1¾oz ball) DK (light worsted) weight yarn:
  10(12) balls of shade Ecru (M)
  1 ball of shade Steel Blue (A)
Pair each of 3.25mm (US 3) and 4mm (US 6) knitting needles
Cable needle

Measurements

To fit ages	3-5	5-7	years
Actual measurements			
Chest	86	94	cm
	33¾	37	in
Length to shoulder	42	45	cm
	16½	17¾	in
Sleeve length	25	30	cm
	10	11¾	in

Tension

20 sts and 28 rows to 10cm/4in square over st st using 4mm (US 6) needles.

Abbreviations

C6B – slip next 3 sts onto cable needle and hold at back of work, k3, then k3 from cable needle.
Cr2L – slip next st onto cable needle and hold at front of work, p1, then k1 from cable needle.
Cr2R – slip next st onto cable needle and hold at back of work, k1, then p1 from cable needle.
C2B – slip next st onto cable needle and hold at back of work, k1, then k1b from cable needle.
C2F – slip next st onto cable needle and hold at front of work, k1b, then k1 from cable needle.
C4B – slip next 2 sts onto cable needle and hold at back of work, k2, then k2 from cable needle.
C4F – slip next 2 sts onto cable needle and hold at front of work, k2, then k2 from cable needle.
k1b – knit into back of st.
p1b – purl into back of st.
Mb – work k1, p1, k1 and p1, into next st, turn, p4, turn, [k2 tog] twice, pass 2nd st over first and off the needle.
See also pages 88 and 95.

PANEL A

(worked over 11 sts)
1st row P3, Cr2R, k1b, Cr2L, p3.
2nd row K3, p1, [k1, p1] twice, k3.
3rd row P2, C2B, p1, k1b, p1, C2F, p2.
4th row K2, p2, k1, p1, k1, p2, k2.
5th row P1, Cr2R, k1b, [p1, k1b] twice, Cr2L, p1.
6th row K1, [p1, k1] 5 times.

7th row P1, Cr2L, k1b, [p1, k1b] twice, Cr2R, p1.

8th row As 4th row.

9th row P2, Cr2L, p1, k1b, p1, Cr2R, p2.

10th row As 2nd row.

11th row P3, Cr2L, k1b, Cr2R, p3.

12th row K4, p3, k4.

13th row P4, sl next 2 sts onto cable needle and leave at back of work, k1, then k1b, k1, from cable needle, p4.

14th row K4, p3, k4.

These 14 rows form the patt and are repeated throughout.

PANEL B

(worked over 18 sts)

1st row P4, Cr2R, k6, Cr2L, p4.

2nd row K4, p1b, k1, p6, k1, p1b, k4.

3rd row P3, Cr2R, p1, k6, p1, Cr2L, p3.

4th row K3, p1b, k2, p6, k2, p1b, k3.

5th row P2, Cr2R, p2, C6B, p2, Cr2L, p2.

6th row K2, p1b, k3, p6, k3, p1b, k2.

7th row P1, Cr2R, p3, k6, p3, Cr2L, p1.

8th row K1, p1b, k4, p6, k4, p1b, k1.

9th row P1, Cr2L, p3, k6, p3, Cr2R, p1.

10th row As 6th row.

11th row P2, Cr2L, p2, C6B, p2, Cr2R, p2.

12th row As 4th row.

13th row P3, Cr2L, p1, k6, p1, Cr2R, p3.

14th row As 2nd row.

15th row P4, Cr2L, k6, Cr2R, p4.

16th row K5, p1b, p6, p1b, k5.

These 16 rows form the patt and are repeated throughout.

PANEL C

(worked over 39 sts)

1st row P7, ★ [Cr2R] twice, p1, [Cr2L] twice, p7; rep from ★ once more.

2nd row K7, ★ p1b, k1, p1b, k3, p1b, k1, p1b, k7; rep from ★ once more.

3rd row P6, ★ [Cr2R] twice, p3, [Cr2L] twice, p5; rep from ★ once more, p1.

4th row K6, ★ p1b, k1, p1b, k5; rep from ★ 3 times more, k1.

5th row P5, ★ [Cr2R] twice, p5, [Cr2L] twice, p3; rep from ★ once more, p2.

6th row K5, ★ p1b, k1, p1b, k7, p1b, k1, p1b, k3; rep from ★

once more, k2.

7th row P4, ★ [Cr2R] twice, p7, [Cr2L] twice, p1; rep from ★ once more, p3.

8th row K4, ★ p1b, k1, p1b, k9, [p1b, k1] twice; rep from ★ once more, k3.

9th row P3, Mb, ★ k1, p1, k1, p9, k1 p1, k1, Mb; rep from ★ once more, p3.

10th row As 8th row.

11th row P4, ★ [Cr2L] twice, p7, [Cr2R] twice, p1; rep from ★ once more, p3.

12th row As 6th row.

13th row P5, ★ [Cr2L] twice, p5, [Cr2R] twice, p3; rep from ★ once more, p2.

14th row As 4th row.

15th row P6, ★ [Cr2L] twice, p3, [Cr2R] twice, p5; rep from ★ once more, p1.

16th row As 2nd row.

17th row P7, ★ [Cr2L] twice, p1, [Cr2R] twice, p7; rep from ★ once more.

18th row K8, ★ p1b, [k1, p1b] 3 times, k9, p1b, [k1, p1b] 3 times, k8.

19th row P8, k1, p1, k1, Mb, k1, p1, k1, p9, k1, p1, k1, Mb, k1, p1, k1, p8.

20th row As 18th row.

These 20 rows form the patt and are repeated throughout.

BACK

With 3.25mm (US 3) needles and yarn A, cast on 111(123) sts.

1st row K3, ★ p2, Cr2R, k1, Cr2L, p2, k3; rep from ★ to end.

2nd row P3, ★ k2, p1, [k1, p1] twice, k2, p3; rep from ★ to end.

Cont in yarn M only.

3rd row K3, ★ p1, Cr2R, p1, k1, p1, Cr2L, p1, k3; rep from ★ to end.

4th row P3, ★ k1, p1, [k2, p1] twice, k1, p3; rep from ★ to end.

5th row K3, ★ Cr2R, p2, k1, p2, Cr2L, k3; rep from ★ to end.

6th row P3, ★ k4, p1, k4, p3; rep from ★ to end.

These 6 rows form the welt patt.

Cont in patt until 36 rows have been worked, inc one st at each end of last row. 113(125) sts.

Change to 4mm (US 6) needles and patt.

1st size only

1st row Work across 1st row of panel A, k4, work across 1st row of panel B, k4, work across 1st row of panel C, k4, work across 1st row of panel B, k4, work across 1st row of panel A.

2nd row Work across 2nd row of panel A, p4, work across 2nd row of panel B, p4, work across 2nd row of panel C, p4, work across 2nd row of panel B, p4, work across 2nd row of panel A.

3rd row Work across 3rd row of panel A, C4F, work across 3rd row of panel B, C4F, work across 3rd row of panel C, C4B, work across 3rd row of panel B, C4B, work across 3rd row of panel A.

4th row Work across 4th row of panel A, p4, work across 4th row of panel B, p4, work across 4th row of panel C, p4, work across 4th row of panel B, p4, work across 4th row of panel A.

These 4 rows form cable panels and set the patt for panels A, B, and C.

2nd size only

1st row P2, k4, work across 1st row of panel A, k4, work across 1st row of panel B, k4, work across 1st row of panel C, k4, work across 1st row of panel B, k4, work across 1st row of panel A, k4, p2.

2nd row K2, p4, work across 2nd row of panel A, p4, work across 2nd row of panel B, p4, work across 2nd row of panel C, p4, work across 2nd row of panel B, p4, work across 2nd row of panel A, p4, k2.

3rd row P2, C4F, work across 3rd row of panel A, C4F, work across 3rd row of panel B, C4F, work across 3rd row of panel C, C4B, work across 3rd row of panel B, C4B, work across 3rd row of panel A, C4B, p2.

4th row K2, p4, work across 4th row of panel A, p4, work across 4th row of panel B, p4, work across 4th row of panel C, p4, work across 4th row of panel B, p4, work across 4th row of panel A, p4, k2.

These 4 rows form cable panels and set the patt for panels A, B, and C.

Both sizes

Patt a further 80(90) rows.

Shape neck

Next row Patt 43(47) sts, turn and work on these sts for first side of neck.

Cast off 3 sts at beg of next and foll alt row. 37(41) sts.

Shape shoulder

Cast off 12(13) sts at beg of next and foll
alt row.

Work 1 row.

Cast off rem 13(15) sts.

With right side facing, slip centre 27(31) sts
onto a holder, rejoin yarn to rem sts, patt
to end.

Complete to match first side.

POCKET LINING (MAKE 1)

With 3.25mm (US 3) needles and yarn M,
cast on 27 sts.

Starting with a k row, work 35 rows in st st.
Leave these sts on a holder.

FRONT

With 3.25mm (US 3) needles and yarn A, cast
on 111(123) sts.

1st row K3, ★ p2, Cr2R, k1, Cr2L, p2, k3; rep
from ★ to end.

2nd row P3, ★ k2, p1, [k1, p1] twice, k2, p3;
rep from ★ to end.

Cont in yarn M only.

3rd row K3, ★ p1, Cr2R, p1, k1, p1, Cr2L, p1,
k3; rep from ★ to end.

4th row P3, ★ k1, p1, [k2, p1] twice, k1, p3;
rep from ★ to end.

5th row K3, ★ Cr2R, p2, k1, p2, Cr2L, k3; rep
from ★ to end.

6th row P3, ★ k4, p1, k4, p3; rep from ★
to end.

These 6 rows form the welt patt.

Cont in patt until 34 rows have been worked.

Next row Patt 72(84) sts in yarn M, patt 27
sts in yarn A, patt 12 sts in yarn M.

Next row Using yarn M, inc in first st, patt
next 11 sts, patt next 27 sts in yarn A and
place these 27 sts on a spare needle, using yarn
M, p across sts of pocket lining, then patt
71(83) sts, inc in last st. 113(125) sts.

Change to 4mm (US 6) needles and patt as
given for Back.

Patt 72(82) rows.

Shape neck

Next row Patt 45(49) sts, turn and work on these sts for first
side of neck.

Dec one st at neck edge, on the next 8 rows. 37(41) sts.

Work 7 rows straight.

Shape shoulder

Cast off 12(13) sts at beg of next and foll alt row.

Work 1 row.

Cast off rem 13(15) sts.

With right side facing, slip centre 23(27) sts onto a holder,
rejoin yarn to rem sts, patt to end.

Complete to match first side.

SLEEVES

Using 3.25mm (US 3) needles and yarn A cast on 59 sts.

1st row K1, p2, Cr2R, k1, Cr2L, p2, ★ k3, p2, Cr2R, k1,
Cr2L, p2; rep from ★ to last st, k1.

2nd row P1, k2, p1, [k1, p1] twice, k2, ★ p3, k2, p1, [k1, p1]
twice, k2; rep from ★ to last st, p1.

Cont in yarn M only. These 2 rows set the welt patt.

Work a further 16 rows, inc 2 sts evenly across row. 61 sts.

Change to 4mm (US 6) needles and patt.

1st row Work across last 7 sts of 1st row of panel B, k4, work
across 1st row of panel C, k4, work across first 7 sts of 1st
row of panel B.

2nd row Work across last 7 sts of 2nd row of panel B, p4,
work across 2nd row of panel C, p4, work across first 7 sts of
2nd row of panel B.

3rd row Work across last 7 sts of 3rd row of panel B, C4F,
work across 3rd row of panel C, C4B, work across first 7 sts
3rd row of panel B.

4th row Work across last 7 sts of 4th row of panel B, p4,
work across 4th row of panel C, p4, work across first 7 sts of
4th row of panel B.

These 4 rows form cable panels and set the patt for panels A,
and B.

Cont in patt **at the same** time inc and work into patt one st
at each end of the next and every foll 4th row until there are
85(91) sts, working inc sts into panel B and 4 st cable panel,
and rem sts in reversed st st.

Cont straight until sleeve measures 25(30)cm/10(11¾)in from
cast on edge, ending with a wrong side row.

Cast off.

NECKBAND

Join right shoulder seam.

With 3.25mm (US 3) needles, right side facing and yarn M, pick up and k18(19) sts down left front neck, k23(27) sts from centre front holder, pick up and k17(18) sts up right side of front neck, 7(8) sts down right side of back neck, k27(31) sts from back neck holder, 7(8) sts up left side of back neck. 99(111) sts.

Next row P3, ★ k4, p1, k4, p3; rep from ★ to end.

Starting with 1st row work 16 rows in welt patt as given for Back.

Change to yarn A.

Work 2 rows in patt.

Cast off loosely in patt.

POCKET TOP

With 3.25mm (US 3) needles, right side facing and yarn A, cast off sts in patt.

MAKE UP

Join left shoulder and neckband. Sew on sleeves. Sew pocket lining in place. Join side and sleeve seams.

BUTTERFLY cardigan

This pretty, summer cardigan with butterfly motifs has a contrasting checked border and rolled edge. Match the colours you have used for the motif with those on the border for a pretty finish.

BACK

With 4mm (US 6) needles and yarn A, cast on 76(80) sts.
Beg with a k row, work 3 rows in st st.
4th row P * 2B, 2C; rep from * to end.
5th row K * 2C, 2B; rep from * to end.
6th row P * 2M, 2B; rep from * to end.
7th row K * 2B, 2M; rep from * to end.
Beg with a p row, work 3(5) rows st st in M.
Work in st st and patt from Chart 1 until row 44(42) has been worked.

Shape armholes

Cast off 3(4) sts at beg of next 2 rows.
70(72) sts.
Cont straight until row 84(88) has been worked.
Cont in M only.

Materials

Debbie Bliss Cotton DK (100% cotton; 84m/91yd per 50g/1¾oz ball) DK (light worsted) weight yarn:
  9(10) balls of shade Duck Egg (M)
  1 ball each of shades:
  Ruby (A)
  Steel Blue (B)
  French Navy (C)
Pair each of 3.75mm (US 5) and 4mm (US 6) knitting needles
7 buttons

Measurements

To fit ages	2	3	years
Actual measurements			
Chest	74	78	cm
	29	30¾	in
Length to shoulder	33	35	cm
	13	13¾	in
Sleeve length	21	24	cm
	8¼	9½	in

Tension

20 sts and 28 rows to 10cm/4in square over st st using 4mm (US 6) needles.

Abbreviations

See page 95.

Note

Read chart from right to left on right side rows and from left to right on wrong side rows (see page 83).
When working motifs, use separate balls of yarn for each area of colour and twist yarns together on wrong side to avoid holes (see page 86).

Shape shoulders

Cast off 10(11) sts at the beg of the next 2 rows and 10 sts at beg of foll 2 rows.
Cast off rem 30 sts.

LEFT FRONT

With 4mm (US 6) needles and A, cast on 37(39) sts.
Beg with a k row, work 3 rows in st st.
4th row P1(3)B, * 2C, 2B; rep from * to end.
5th row K * 2B, 2C; rep from * to last 1(3) sts, 1(3)B.
6th row P1(3)M, * 2B, 2M; rep from * to end.
7th row K * 2M, 2B; rep from * to last 1(3) sts, 1(3)M.
Beg with a p row, work 3(5) rows st st in M.
Work in st st and patt from Chart 1 until row 44(42) has been worked.

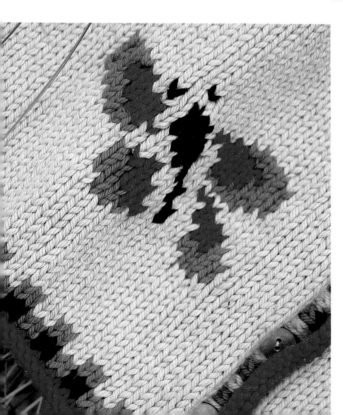

Shape armhole

Cast off 3(4) sts at beg of next row. 34(35) sts.
Cont in st st and patt from Chart 1 until row
57(60) has been worked.

Shape front

Dec one st at front edge on next 4 rows and
every foll alt row until 20(21) sts rem.
Cont straight until row 84(88) of Chart 1 has
been worked.
Cont in M only.

Shape shoulder

Cast off 10 (11) sts at the beg of the next row.
Work 1 row.
Cast off rem 10 sts.

RIGHT FRONT

With 4mm (US 6) needles and A, cast on
37(39) sts.
Beg with a k row, work 3 rows in st st.
4th row P ★ 2C, 2B; rep from ★ to last 1(3)
sts, 1(3)C.
5th row K1(3)C, ★ 2B, 2C; rep from ★ to end.
6th row P ★ 2B, 2M; rep from ★ to last 1(3)
sts, 1(3)B.
7th row K1(3)B, ★ 2M, 2B; rep from ★ to
end.
Beg with a p row, work 3(5) rows st st in M.
Work in st st and patt from Chart 1 until row
45(43) has been worked.

Shape armhole

Cast off 3(4) sts at beg of next row. 34(35) sts.
Cont in st st and patt from Chart 1 until row
57(60) has been worked.

Shape front

Dec one st at front edge on next 4 rows and
every foll alt row until 20(21) sts rem.
Cont straight until row 84(88) of Chart 1 has
been worked.
Cont in M only.
Work 1 row.

Shape shoulder

Cast off 10 (11) sts at the beg of the next row.
Work 1 row.
Cast off rem 10 sts.

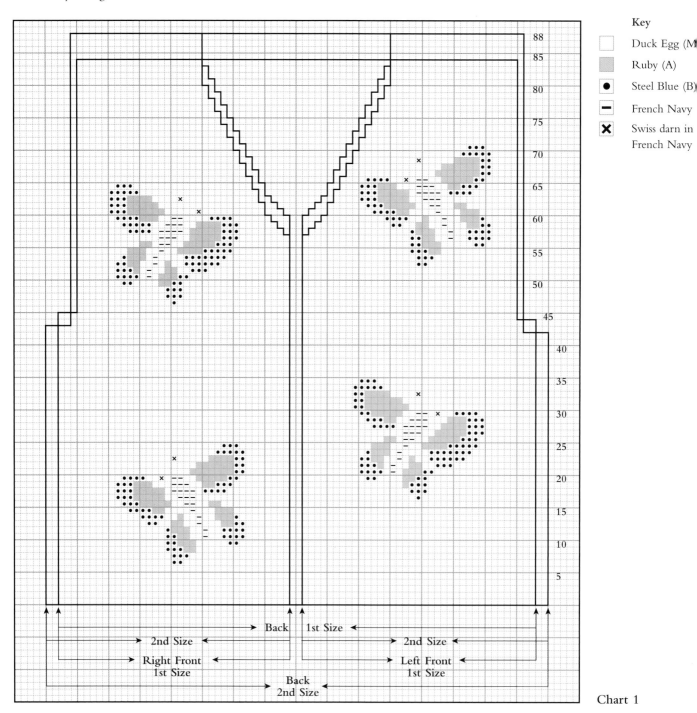

Key

☐	Duck Egg (M)
▨	Ruby (A)
●	Steel Blue (B)
—	French Navy
✕	Swiss darn in French Navy

Chart 1

SLEEVES

With 4mm (US 6) needles and A, cast on 36(40) sts.

Beg with a k row, work 3 rows in st st.

4th row P ★ 2B, 2C; rep from ★ to end.

5th row K ★ 2C, 2B; rep from ★ to end.

6th row P ★ 2M, 2B; rep from ★ to end.

7th row K ★ 2B, 2M; rep from ★ to end.

Beg with a p row, work 1(5) rows st st in M.

Cont in patt from Chart 2 **at the same time** inc one st at each end of the 6th and every foll 5th row until there are 56(62) sts.

Cont straight until row 62(66) of Chart 2 has been worked. Cast off.

FRONTBAND

Join shoulder seams.

With right side facing, using 3.75mm (US 5) needles and M, pick up and k51(55) sts along left front to beg of neck shaping, 18(20) sts to shoulder, 30 sts across back neck, 18(20) sts to beg of neck shaping and 51(55) sts along right front. 168(180) sts.

Chart 2

P 1 row.

1st row K ★ 2M, 2B; rep from ★ to end.

2nd row P ★ 2B, 2M; rep from ★ to end.

3rd row (Buttonhole row) K2B, (yf, k2togC, k2B, k2C, k2B] 6 times, yf, k2togC, ★k2B, k2C; rep from ★ to end.

4th row P ★ 2C, 2B; rep from ★ to end.

Change to A.

Beg with a k row, work 3 rows in st st.

Cast off.

MAKE UP

Sew on sleeves, sewing last 4(6) rows to sts cast off underarm, placing centre of sleeves to shoulder seams. Join side and sleeve seams. Sew on buttons. Swiss darn butterfly antenna in C as shown on Chart.

SNOWFLAKE AND heart baby throw

For a soft throw for a winter baby,
cotton is great next to the skin.
The snowflake and heart motifs
are inspired by a Nordic theme
and worked in a cool cream and
pale blue. The hearts are
decorated with simple embroidery.

Materials
Debbie Bliss Cotton DK (100% cotton; 84m/91yd per
50g/1¾oz ball) DK (light worsted) weight yarn:
 8 balls of shade Ecru (M)
 2 balls of shade Steel Blue (A)
Pair of 4mm (US 6) knitting needles

Measurements
Approximately 61cm x 75cm/24in x 29½in.

Tension
20 sts and 28 rows to 10cm/4in square over st st using
4mm (US 6) needles.

Abbreviations
See page 95.

Note
Read chart from right to left on right side rows and from
left to right on wrong side rows (see page 83).
When working motifs, use separate balls of yarn for each
area of colour and twist yarns together on wrong side to
avoid holes (see page 86).
Embroidery for Motif C (see page 90).

TO MAKE
Using yarn M, cast on 128 sts.
K 5 rows.
Cont in patt as folls:
1st row K2, patt across 1st row of Motif A,
k2, patt across 1st row of Motif B, k2, patt
across 1st row of Motif C, k2, patt across
1st row of Motif B, k2, patt across 1st row
of Motif D, k2, patt across 1st row of
Motif B, k2.
2nd row K2, patt across 2nd row of Motif B, k2,
patt across 2nd row of Motif D, k2, patt across
2nd row of Motif B, k2, patt across 2nd row of
Motif C, k2, patt across 2nd row of Motif B,
k2, patt across 2nd row of Motif A, k2.
These 2 rows set the patt.
Cont in patt until 24 rows of motifs have
been worked.
25th to 28th rows K to end.
29th row K2, patt across 1st row of
Motif B, k2, patt across 1st row of Motif C,
k2, patt across 1st row of Motif B, k2, patt
across 1st row of Motif D, k2, patt across
1st row of Motif B, k2, patt across 1st row of
Motif A, k2.
30th row K2, patt across 2nd row of
Motif A, k2, patt across 2nd row of Motif B,
k2, patt across 2nd row of Motif D, k2, patt
across 2nd row of Motif B, k2, patt across
2nd row of Motif C, k2, patt across 2nd row
of Motif B, k2.
These 2 rows set the patt.

Cont in patt until 24 rows of motifs have
been worked.
53rd to 56th rows K to end.
57th row K2, patt across 1st row of
Motif C, k2, patt across 1st row of Motif B,
k2, patt across 1st row of Motif D, k2, patt
across 1st row of Motif B, k2, patt across
1st row of Motif A, k2, patt across 1st row of
Motif B, k2.
58th row K2, patt across 2nd row of
Motif B, k2, patt across 2nd row of Motif A,
k2, patt across 2nd row of Motif B, k2, patt
across 2nd row of Motif D, k2, patt across
2nd row of Motif B, k2, patt across 2nd row of
Motif C, k2.
These 2 rows set the patt.
Cont in patt until 24 rows of motifs have
been worked.
81st to 84th rows K to end.
85th row K2, patt across 1st row of
Motif B, k2, patt across 1st row of Motif D,
k2, patt across 1st row of Motif B, k2, patt
across 1st row of Motif A, k2, patt across
1st row of Motif B, k2, patt across 1st row of
Motif C, k2.

Motif A

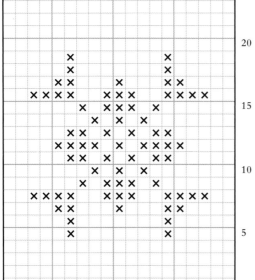

19

Motif B

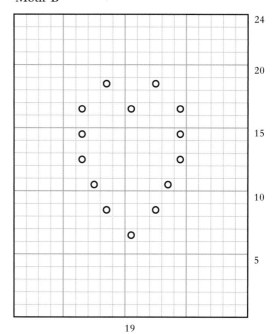

19

Motif C

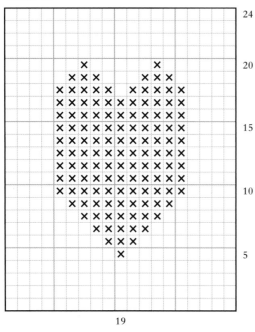

19

Motif D

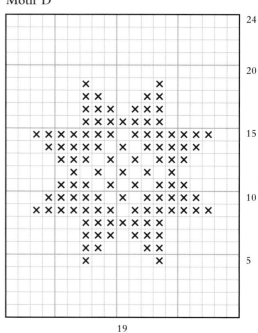

19

Key

☐ Ecru (M)

✗ Steel Blue (A)

○ Mb – Using yarn M, k into front, back and front of next st, turn, p3, turn, sl1, k2 tog, psso

1st row of Motif A, k2, patt across 1st row of Motif B, k2, patt across 1st row of Motif C, k2, patt across 1st row of Motif B, k2, patt across 1st row of Motif D, k2.

142nd row K2, patt across 2nd row of Motif D, k2, patt across 2nd row of Motif B, k2, patt across 2nd row of Motif C, k2, patt across 2nd row of Motif B, k2, patt across 2nd row of Motif A, k2, patt across row 2 of Motif B, k2.

These 2 rows set the patt.

Cont in patt until 24 rows of motifs have been worked.

165th to 168th rows K to end.

169th to 220th rows As 1st to 52nd rows.

221st to 226th rows K to end.

Cast off.

TO COMPLETE

Using yarn M, work 5 lazy daisy stitches on each heart on Motif C (see page 90).

Using yarn A, make 4 pom-poms and sew one to each corner.

86th row K2, patt across 2nd row of Motif C, k2, patt across 2nd row of Motif B, k2, patt across 2nd row of Motif A, k2, patt across 2nd row of Motif B, k2, patt across 2nd row of Motif D, k2, patt across 2nd row of Motif B, k2.

These 2 rows set the patt.

Cont in patt until 24 rows of motifs have been worked.

109th to 112nd rows K to end.

113th row K2, patt across 1st row of Motif D, k2, patt across 1st row of Motif B, k2, patt across 1st row of Motif A, k2, patt across 1st row of Motif B, k2, patt across 1st row of Motif C, k2, patt across 1st row of Motif B, k2.

114th row K2, patt across 2nd row of Motif B, k2, patt across 2nd row of Motif C, k2, patt across 2nd row of Motif B, k2, patt across 2nd row of Motif A, k2, patt across 2nd row of Motif B, k2, patt across 2nd row of Motif D, k2.

These 2 rows set the patt.

Cont in patt until 24 rows of motifs have been worked.

137th to 140th rows K to end.

141st row K2, patt across 1st row of Motif B, k2, patt across

RUGBY shirt

Based on the classic British rugby shirt, this design has multi-coloured stripes contrasted against a crisp, white collar. Stripes are fun to knit, particularly if you want to avoid complicated colour techniques.

Materials

Debbie Bliss Cotton DK (100% cotton; 84m/91yd per 50g/1¾oz ball) DK (light worsted) weight yarn:
2(3:3) balls of shade White (M)
2(2:3) balls each of shades:
Duck Egg (A)
Leaf (B)
Pale Pink (C)
2 balls of shade Steel Blue (D)
1 ball each of shades:
French Navy (E)
Ruby (F)
Putty (G)
Pair each of 3.25mm (US 3) and 4mm (US 6) knitting needles

Measurements

To fit ages	1-2	2-3	3-4	years
Actual measurements				
Chest	70	74	80	cm
	27½	29	31½	in
Length to shoulder	36	40	43	cm
	14¼	15¾	17	in
Sleeve length	22	24	28	cm
	8¾	9½	11	in

Tension

20 sts and 28 rows to 10cm/4in square over st st using 4mm (US 6) needles.

Abbreviations

See page 95.

Stripe patt: 3 rows yarn A, 3 rows yarn B, 1 row yarn M, 2 rows yarn G, 3 rows yarn C, 2 rows yarn F, 1 row yarn M, 4 rows yarn D, 1 row yarn E and 1 row yarn M.

BACK

With 3.25mm (US 3) needles and yarn A, cast on 70(74:82) sts.
1st rib row K2, ★ p2, k2; rep from ★ to end.
2nd rib row P2, ★ k2, p2; rep from ★ to end.

Rep the last 2 rows once more, inc 2(2:0) sts evenly across last row. 72(76:82) sts.
Change to 4mm (US 6) needles.
Beg with a k row cont in st st and stripe patt until back measures 36(40:43)cm/14¼(15¾:17)in from cast on edge, ending with a p row.

Shape shoulders

Cast off 12(12:13) sts at beg of next 2 rows and 11(12:13) sts on foll 2 rows.
Leave rem 26(28:30) sts on a holder.

FRONT

Work as given for Back until front measures 25(28:31)cm/10(11:12¼)in from cast on edge, ending with a p row.

Divide for front opening

Next row K34(36:39), turn and work on these sts for first side of front neck. Work 5(6:6)cm/2(2¼:2¼)in straight, ending at side edge.

Shape neck

Next row K to last 6(7:8) sts, leave these sts on a safety pin.

Dec one st at neck edge on every row until 23(24:26) sts rem.

Work straight until front measures the same as Back to shoulder, ending at side edge.

Shape shoulder

Cast off 12(12:13) sts at beg of next row.
Work 1 row. Cast off rem 11(12:13) sts.
With right side facing, join on yarn, cast off centre 4 sts, k to end.
Complete to match first side of neck.

SLEEVES

Using 3.25mm (US 3) needles and yarn A, cast on 38(38:42) sts.
Work 4(5:5)cm/1½(2:2)in rib as given for Back, ending with a right side row.
Inc row Rib 4(5:4), ★ m1, rib 6(4:7); rep from ★ to last 4(5:3) sts, m1, rib 4(5:3). 44(46:48) sts.
Change to 4mm (US 6) needles.
Beg with a k row and working in stripe patt as before, inc one st at each end of the 3rd and every foll 4th(4th:5th) row until there are 64(68:72) sts.
Cont straight until sleeve measures 22(24:28)cm/8¾(9½:11)in from cast on edge, ending with a p row.
Cast off.

LEFT FRONT BAND

With right side facing, 3.25mm (US 3) needles and yarn M, pick up and k16 sts down left side of front neck.
1st row K1, [p2, k2] 3 times, p2, k1.
2nd row K3, [p2, k2] twice, p2, k3.
Rep the last 2 rows once more and the 1st row again.
Cast off in rib.

RIGHT FRONT BAND

With right side facing, 3.25mm (US 3) needles and yarn M, pick up and k16 sts up right side of front neck.

Work 5 rows rib as given for Left Front Band.

COLLAR

Join shoulder seams.

With right side facing, 3.25mm (US 3) needles and yarn M, slip 6(7:8) sts from safety pin on right front neck onto a needle, pick up and k15(15:17) sts up right side of front neck, k26(28:30) sts from back neck holder, pick up and k15(15:17) sts down left side of front neck, k6(7:8) sts from safety pin on left front neck. 68(72:80) sts.

1st row K1, [p2, k2] 16(17:19) times, p2, k1.

Cont in rib as for Left Front Band.

Next 2 rows Rib to last 20 sts, turn.

Next 2 rows Rib to last 16 sts, turn.

Next 2 rows Rib to last 12 sts, turn.

Next 2 rows Rib to last 8 sts, turn.

Next row Rib to last 5 sts, p2, k3.

Work a further 16 rows in rib.

Cast off.

TO MAKE UP

Sew on sleeves. Join side and sleeve seams. Place lower edge of right front band over lower edge of left front band and sew in place.

LACE AND BOBBLE throw

This throw uses the same stitch patterns as the Guernsey Dress on page 32 and the Lace and Bobble Bootees on page 38, so all the designs together would make a lovely gift set for a nearly-new baby. The throw is the ideal size for a buggy or small pram.

Materials

Debbie Bliss Baby Cashmerino (55% wool, 33% acrylic, 12% cashmere; 125m/137yd per 50g/1¾oz ball) light DK (sport) weight yarn:
  6 balls of shade Ecru
Pair of 3.25mm (US 3) knitting needles
Cable needle

Measurements

Approximately 58cm x 68cm/23in x 26¾in.

Tension

25 sts and 34 rows to 10cm/4in square over st st using 3.25mm (US 3) needles.

Abbreviations

Mb – work k1, p1, k1, p1, k1, into next st, turn, p5, turn, pass 2nd, 3rd, 4th and 5th st over first and off the needle, then pass st back onto right hand needle.
C4F – slip next 2 sts onto cable needle and hold at front of work, k2, then k2 from cable needle.
Also see pages 88 and 95.

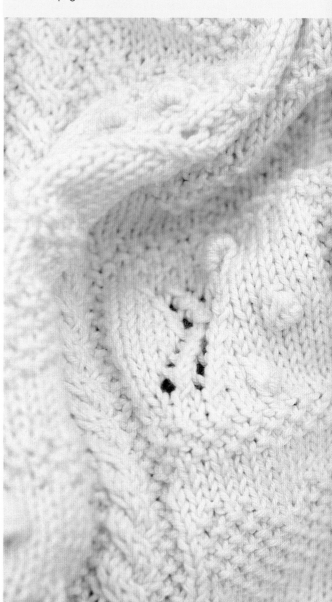

PANEL A

(worked over 15 sts)
1st row K to end.
2nd row P to end.
3rd row K7, p1, k7.
4th row P6, k1, p1, k1, p6.
5th row K5, p1, [k1, p1] twice, k5.
6th row P4, k1, [p1, k1] 3 times, p4.
7th row K3, p1, [k1, p1] 4 times, k3.
8th row P2, k1, [p1, k1] 5 times, p2.
9th row K1, [p1, k1] 7 times.
10th row As 8th row.
11th row As 9th row.
12th row As 8th row.
13th row [K1, p1] 3 times, k3, [p1, k1] 3 times.
14th row P2, k1, p1, k1, p5, k1, p1, k1, p2.
15th row K to end.
16th row P to end.
17th row K to end.
18th row P to end.
These 18 rows form the patt panel.

PANEL B

(worked over 15 sts)
1st row K to end.
2nd and alt rows P to end.
3rd row K to end.
5th row K6, k2 tog, yf, k7.
7th row K5, k2 tog, yf, k1, yf, skpo, k5.
9th row K4, k2 tog, yf, k3, yf, skpo, k4.
11th row K3, k2 tog, yf, k2, Mb, k2, yf, skpo, k3.
13th row K2, k2 tog, yf, k7, yf, skpo, k2.
15th row K1, k2 tog, yf, k2, Mb, k3, Mb, k2, yf, skpo, k1.

17th row K to end.
18th row P to end.
These 18 rows form the patt panel.

PANEL C

(worked over 15 sts)
1st row K to end.
2nd and alt rows P to end.
3rd row K6, Mb, k2, [k2 tog, yf] twice, k2.
5th row K8, [k2 tog, yf] twice, k3.
7th row K7, [k2 tog, yf] twice, k4.
9th row K3, Mb, k2, [k2 tog, yf] twice, k5.
11th row K7, [yf, skpo] twice, k4.
13th row K8, [yf, skpo] twice, k3.
15th row K6, Mb, k2, [yf, skpo] twice, k2.
17th row K to end.
18th row P to end.
These 18 rows form the patt panel.

TO MAKE

With 3.25mm (US 3) needles cast on 146 sts.
1st row ★ K1, [p1, k1] 10 times, C4F; rep from ★ to last 21 sts, k1, [p1, k1] 10 times.
2nd row ★ K1, [p1, k1] 10 times, p4; rep from ★ to last 21 sts, k1, [p1, k1] 10 times.
3rd row ★ K1, [p1, k1] 10 times, k4; rep from ★ to last 21 sts, k1, [p1, k1] 10 times.
4th row ★ K1, [p1, k1] 10 times, p4; rep from ★ to last 21 sts, k1, [p1, k1] 10 times.
These 4 rows form cable and moss st panel.
Patt 2 more rows.
7th row Moss st 3, work 1st row of patt panel B, patt 10, work 1st row of patt panel A, patt 10, work 1st row of patt panel C, patt 10, work 1st row of patt panel A, patt 10, work 1st row of patt panel B, patt 10, work 1st row of patt panel A, moss st 3.
8th row Moss st 3, work 2nd row of patt panel A, patt 10, work 2nd row of patt panel B, patt 10, work 2nd row of patt panel A, patt 10, work 2nd row of patt panel C, patt 10, work 2nd row of patt panel A, patt 10, work 2nd row of patt panel B, moss st 3.
9th to 24th rows Rep 7th and 8th rows eight times, working 3rd to 18th rows of patt panels.
25th row ★ K1, [p1, k1] 10 times, C4F; rep from ★ to last 21 sts, k1, [p1, k1] 10 times.
26th row ★ K1, [p1, k1] 10 times, p4; rep from ★ to last 21 sts, k1, [p1, k1] 10 times.

27th row ★ K1, [p1, k1] 10 times, k4; rep from ★ to last 21 sts, k1, [p1, k1] 10 times.
28th row ★ K1, [p1, k1] 10 times, p4; rep from ★ to last 21 sts, k1, [p1, k1] 10 times.
29th row Moss st 3, work 1st row of patt panel A, patt 10, work 1st row of patt panel C, patt 10, work 1st row of patt panel A, patt 10, work 1st row of patt panel B, patt 10, work 1st row of patt panel A, patt 10, work 1st row of patt panel C, moss st 3.
30th row Moss st 3, work 2nd row of patt panel C, patt 10, work 2nd row of patt panel A, patt 10, work 2nd row of patt panel B, patt 10, work 2nd row of patt panel A, patt 10, work 2nd row of patt panel C, patt 10, work 2nd row of patt panel A, moss st 3.
31st to 46th rows Rep 29th and 30th rows eight times, working 3rd to 18th rows of patt panels.
47th row ★ K1, [p1, k1] 10 times, k4; rep from ★ to last 21 sts, k1, [p1, k1] 10 times.
48th row ★ K1, [p1, k1] 10 times, p4; rep from ★ to last 21 sts, k1, [p1, k1] 10 times.
49th row ★ K1, [p1, k1] 10 times, C4F; rep from ★ to last 21 sts, k1, [p1, k1] 10 times.
50th row ★ K1, [p1, k1] 10 times, p4; rep from ★ to last 21 sts, k1, [p1, k1] 10 times.
51st row Moss st 3, work 1st row of patt panel C, patt 10, work 1st row of patt panel A, patt 10, work 1st row of patt panel B, patt 10, work 1st row of patt panel A, patt 10, work 1st row of patt panel C, patt 10, work 1st row of patt panel A, moss st 3.
52nd row Moss st 3, work 2nd row of patt panel A, patt 10, work 2nd row of patt panel C, patt 10, work 2nd row of patt panel A, patt 10, work 2nd row of patt panel B, patt 10, work 2nd row of patt panel A, patt 10, work 2nd row of patt panel C, moss st 3.
53rd to 68th rows Rep 51st and 52nd rows eight times, working 3rd to 18th rows of patt panels.
69th row ★ K1, [p1, k1] 10 times, C4F; rep from ★ to last 21 sts, k1, [p1, k1] 10 times.
70th row ★ K1, [p1, k1] 10 times, p4; rep from ★ to last 21 sts, k1, [p1, k1] 10 times.
71st row ★ K1, [p1, k1] 10 times, k4; rep from ★ to last 21 sts, k1, [p1, k1] 10 times.
72nd row ★ K1, [p1, k1] 10 times, p4; rep from ★ to last 21 sts, k1, [p1, k1] 10 times.
73rd row Moss st 3, work 1st row of patt panel A, patt 10, work 1st row of patt panel B, patt 10, work 1st row of patt panel A, patt 10, work 1st row of patt panel C, patt 10, work 1st row of patt panel A, patt 10, work 1st row of patt panel B, moss st 3.
74th row Moss st 3, work 2nd row of patt panel B, patt 10,

work 2nd row of patt panel A, patt 10, work 2nd row of patt panel C, patt 10, work 2nd row of patt panel A, patt 10, work 2nd row of patt panel B, patt 10, work 2nd row of patt panel A, moss st 3.

75th to 90th rows Rep 73rd and 74th rows eight times, working 3rd to 18th rows of patt panels.

91st row ★ K1, [p1, k1] 10 times, k4; rep from ★ to last 21 sts, k1, [p1, k1] 10 times.

92nd row ★ K1, [p1, k1] 10 times, p4; rep from ★ to last 21 sts, k1, [p1, k1] 10 times.

93rd row ★ K1, [p1, k1] 10 times, C4F; rep from ★ to last 21 sts, k1, [p1, k1] 10 times.

94th row ★ K1, [p1, k1] 10 times, p4; rep from ★ to last 21 sts, k1, [p1, k1] 10 times.

95th to 182nd rows Work as given for 7th to 94th rows.
183rd to 248th rows Work as given for 7th to 72nd rows.

249th row ★ K1, [p1, k1] 10 times, C4F; rep from ★ to last 21 sts, k1, [p1, k1] 10 times.
250th row ★ K1, [p1, k1] 10 times, p4; rep from ★ to last 21 sts, k1, [p1, k1] 10 times.
Cast off.

STRIPED sweater

A simple top with stripes that has a square, nautical-style neckline and neat side vents. The buttoned shoulder fastening makes it easy to pull on and off over a small child's head. It is a perfect design for the fairly new knitter.

Materials
Debbie Bliss Baby Cashmerino (55% wool, 33% acrylic, 12% cashmere; 125m/137yd per 50g/1¾oz ball) light DK (sport) weight yarn:
  3(4:5:6) balls of shade White (M)
  1(1:2:2) balls of shade Kingfisher (A)
Pair each of 2.75mm (US 2) and 3.25mm (US 3) knitting needles
2 small buttons

Measurements

To fit ages	6-12	12-18	18-24	24-36	months
Actual measurements					
Chest	56	62	68	74	cm
	22	24½	26¾	29	in
Length to shoulder	28	31	34	38	cm
	11	12¼	13½	15	in
Sleeve length	16	18	21	24	cm
	6¼	7	8¼	9½	in

Tension
25 sts and 34 rows to 10cm/4in square over st st using 3.25mm (US 3) needles.

Abbreviations
See page 95.

BACK
With 2.75mm (US 2) needles and yarn M, cast on 72(80:86:94) sts.
K 7 rows to form garter st hem.
Change to 3.25mm (US 3) needles.
1st row With yarn M, k to end.
2nd row With yarn M, k3, p to last 3 sts, k3.
3rd row With yarn M, k to end.
4th row With yarn M, k3, p to last 3 sts, k3.
5th row With yarn M, k3, with yarn A, k to last 3 sts, with yarn M, k3.
6th row With yarn M, k3, with yarn A, p to last 3 sts, with yarn M, k3.
Beg with a k row work in st st across all sts and stripe patt of [2 rows yarn M, 2 rows yarn A] twice, 4 rows yarn M and 2 rows yarn A until 42(42:56:56) rows have been worked in striped patt from top of garter st hem.
Cont in st st and yarn M only until back measures 24(27:30:34)cm/9½(10¾:11¾:13½)in from cast on edge, ending with a wrong side row.

Shape shoulders and back neck
Next row K21(24:27:30) sts, turn and work on this set of sts only.

Cont straight until back measures 27(30:33:37)cm/10¾(12:13:14¾)in from cast on edge, ending with a wrong side row.
Change to 2.75mm (US 2) needles.
With yarn M, k 3 rows.
Cast off.
With right side facing, slip centre 30(32:32:34) sts onto a holder, join on yarn, patt to end.
Cont straight until back measures 27(30:33:37)cm/10¾(12:13:14¾)in from cast on edge, ending with a wrong side row.
Change to 2.75mm(US 2) needles.
With yarn M, k 5 rows.
Cast off.

FRONT

Work as given for Back until front measures 22(25:28:31)cm/8¾(10:11¼:12¼)in from cast on edge, ending with a wrong side row.

Shape shoulders and front neck

Next row K21(24:27:30) sts, turn and work on this set of sts only.
Cont straight until front measures same as Back to shoulder, ending with a wrong side row.

Shape shoulder

Change to 2.75mm (US 2) needles.
K 2 rows.
Buttonhole row K14(16:18:20), k2tog, yf, k to end.
K 2 rows.
Cast off.
With right side facing, slip centre 30(32:32:34) sts onto a holder, join on yarn, k to end.
Cont straight until front measures same as Back to shoulder, ending with a wrong side row.
Change to 2.75mm (US 2) needles.
With yarn M, k 3 rows.
Cast off.

SLEEVES

With 2.75mm (US 2) needles and yarn M, cast on 46(46:50:50) sts.
1st row K2, ★ p2, k2; rep from ★ to end.
2nd row P2, ★ k2, p2; rep from ★ to end.
Rep the last 2 rows for 2(2:3:3)cm/¾(¾:1¼:1¼)in, ending with a 2nd row.
Change to 3.25mm (US 3) needles.
Beg with a k row, cont in st st and stripe sequence of 4 rows yarn M, [2 rows yarn A, 2 rows yarn M] twice, and 2 rows yarn A, **at the same time** inc one st at each end of the 3rd and every foll 4th row until there are 62(68:74:78) sts.
Cont straight until sleeve measures 16(18:21:24)cm/¼(7:8¼:9½)in.
Cast off.

BACK NECKBAND

With 2.75mm (US 2) needles and yarn M and right side facing, pick up and k7 sts down right side of back neck, k30(32:32:34) sts from back neck, pick up and k9 sts up left side of back neck. 46(48:48:50) sts. K 1 row.

Dec row K5, skpo, k2 tog, k26(28:28:30), skpo, k2 tog, k7. K 1 row.

Dec row K4, skpo, k2 tog, k24(26:26:28), skpo, k2 tog, k6. K 1 row. Cast off, dec as before.

FRONT NECKBAND

With 2.75mm (US 2) needles and yarn M and right side facing, pick up and k14 sts down left side of front neck, k30(32:32:34) sts from front neck, pick up and k12 sts up right side of front neck. 56(58:58:60) sts. K 1 row.

Dec row K2, k2 tog, yf, k8, skpo, k2 tog, k26(28:28:30), skpo, k2 tog, k10. K 1 row.

Dec row K11, skpo, k2 tog, k24(26:26:30), skpo, k2 tog, k9. K 1 row. Cast off, dec as before.

MAKE UP

Join right shoulder seam. Lap left front buttonhole band over left back button band and catch side edges together. Sew on sleeves. Join side and sleeve seams to top of side slit. Sew on buttons.

SCANDINAVIAN jacket

A generous, zipped jacket based on the classic Scandinavian knitwear designs of bold navy and white patterning with a hint of colour. The Fair Isle and intarsia techniques used here are for the more experienced knitter.

Materials

Debbie Bliss Cotton DK (100% cotton; 84m/91yd per 50g/1¾oz ball) DK (light worsted) weight yarn:
  6(7) balls of shade White (M)
  3 balls of shade French Navy (A)
  2 balls each of shades:
  Ruby (B)
  Steel Blue (C)
Pair each of 3.25mm (US 3) and 4mm (US 6) knitting needles
40(45)cm/16(18)in open-ended zipper

Measurements

To fit ages	5-6	7-8	years
Actual measurements			
Chest	89	97	cm
	35	38	in
Length to shoulder	48	54	cm
	19	21¼	in
Sleeve length	30	35	cm
	11¾	13¾	in

Tension

21 sts and 26 rows to 10cm/4in square over patt using 4mm (US 6) needles.

Abbreviations

See page 95.

Note

Read chart from right to left on right side rows and from left to right on wrong side rows (see page 83).
When working in patt, strand yarn not in use loosely across wrong side of work (see page 84).
When working motifs, use separate balls of yarn for each area of colour and twist yarns together on wrong side to avoid holes (see page 86).

BACK

With 3.25mm (US 3) needles and yarn B cast on 94(102) sts.
1st rib row K2, ★ p2, k2; rep from ★ to end.
Cont in yarn M only.
2nd rib row P2, ★ k2, p2; rep from ★ to end.
Rep the last 2 rows 6(7) times more, inc 2 sts evenly across last row. 96(104) sts.
Change to 4mm (US 6) needles.
Beg with a k row cont in st st.
Work 2(4) rows.
Work in patt from Chart to end of row 80.
Rep from row 50 until back measures 48(54)cm/19(21¼)in from cast on edge, ending with a p row.

Shape Shoulders

Cast off 11(12) sts at beg of next 4 rows and 10(11) sts at beg of foll 2 rows.
Cast off rem 32(34) sts.

LEFT FRONT

With 3.25mm (US 3) needles and yarn B cast on 48(52)sts.
1st rib row K2, ★ p2, k2; rep from ★ to last 6 sts, p2, k4.
Working 2 sts at front edge in yarn B and garter st, and twisting yarns tog at back of work to avoid a hole, cont as folls:
2nd rib row K2 in yarn B, using yarn M, p2, ★ k2, p2; rep from ★ to end.
3rd rib row Using yarn M, k2, ★ p2, k2; rep from ★ to last 2 sts, k2 in yarn B.

4th rib row K2 in yarn B, using yarn M, p2, ★ k2, p2; rep from ★ to end.
Rep the last 2 rows 5(6) times more.
Change to 4mm (US 6) needles.
Next row Using yarn M, k to last 2 sts, k2 in yarn B.
Next row K2 in yarn B, using yarn M, p to end.
Rep the last 2 rows 0(1) times more.
Work in patt from Chart to match Back as folls:
1st row Work across 1st row of Chart, k2 in yarn B.
2nd row K2 in yarn B, work across 2nd row of Chart.

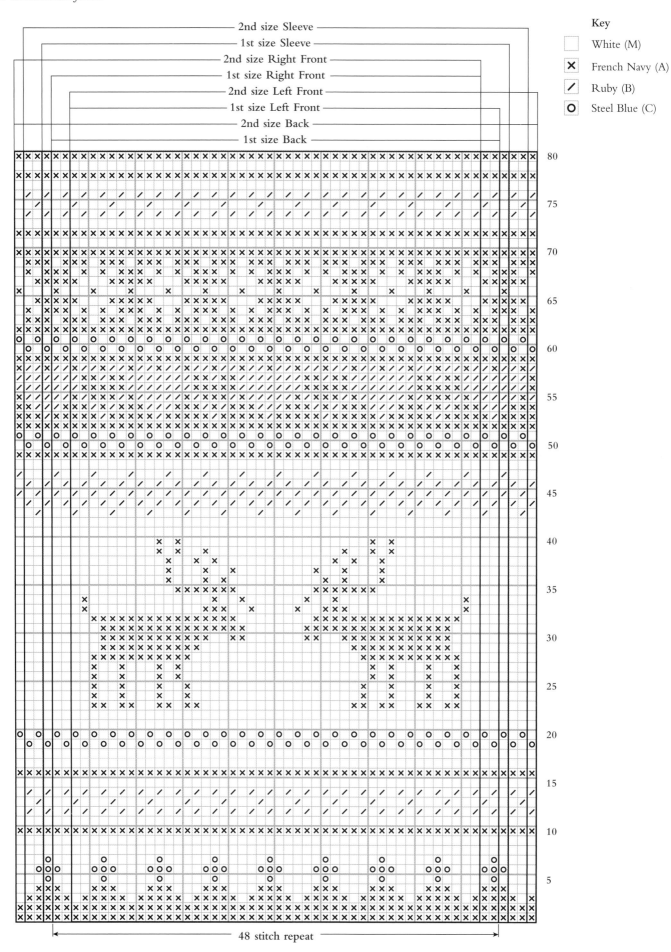

Key

- ☐ White (M)
- ☒ French Navy (A)
- ✎ Ruby (B)
- ⊙ Steel Blue (C)

2nd size Sleeve
1st size Sleeve
2nd size Right Front
1st size Right Front
2nd size Left Front
1st size Left Front
2nd size Back
1st size Back

48 stitch repeat

Cont in patt until work measures 43(48)cm/17(19)in from cast on edge, ending with a wrong side row.

Shape neck

Next row Patt to last 6(8) sts, leave these sts on a safety pin. Dec one st at neck edge on every row until 32(35) sts rem. Cont straight until front matches Back to shoulder shaping, ending at side edge.

Shape shoulder

Cast off 11(12) sts at beg of next and foll alt row.
Work 1 row.
Cast off rem 10(11) sts.

RIGHT FRONT

With 3.25mm (US 3) needles and yarn B cast on 48(52) sts.
1st rib row K4, ★ p2, k2; rep from ★ to end.
Working 2 sts at front edge in yarn B and garter st, and twisting yarns tog at back of work to avoid a hole, cont as folls:
2nd rib row Using yarn M, p2, ★ k2, p2; rep from ★ to last 2 sts, k2 in yarn B.
3rd rib row K2 in yarn B, using yarn M, k2, ★ p2, k2; rep from ★ to end.
4th rib row Using yarn M, p2, ★ k2, p2; rep from ★ to last 2 sts, k2 in yarn B.
Rep the last 2 rows 5(6) times more.
Change to 4mm (US 6) needles.
Next row K2 in yarn B, using yarn M, k to end.
Next row Using yarn M, p to last 2 sts, k2 in yarn B.
Rep the last 2 rows 0(1) times more.
Complete to match Left Front.

SLEEVES

With 3.25mm (US 3) needles and yarn B cast on 46(50) sts.
1st rib row K2, ★ p2, k2; rep from ★ to end.
Cont in yarn M only.
2nd rib row P2, ★ k2, p2; rep from ★ to end.
Rep the last 2 rows 6(7) times more, inc 4 sts evenly across last row. 50(54) sts.
Change to 4mm (US 6) needles.
Beg with a k row cont in st st.
Work 2(4) rows.
Work in patt from Chart, **at the same time** inc one st at each end of next row, then on every 3rd and 4th row alternately until there are 84(94) sts.
Cont straight until sleeve measures 30(35)cm/11¾(13¾)in from cast on edge, ending with a wrong side row.
Cast off.

COLLAR

Join shoulder seams.
With 3.25mm (US 3) needles right sides facing and yarn A, slip 6(8) sts from holder onto a needle, pick up and k15(16) sts up right front neck, 32(34) sts from back neck, 15(16) sts down left front neck, k6(8) sts from holder. 74(82) sts.
1st row (right side) K4, ★ p2, k2; rep from ★ to last 6 sts, p2, k4.
2nd row K2, ★ p2, k2; rep from ★ to end.
These 2 rows set the rib patt with garter st border.
Next 2 rows Rib to last 18 sts, turn.
Next 2 rows Rib to last 14 sts, turn.
Next 2 rows Rib to last 10 sts, turn.
Next 2 rows Rib to last 8 sts, turn.
Rib to end.
Work a further 7(8)cm/2¾(3¼)in in rib patt, ending with a wrong side row.
Change to yarn C.
Rib 1 row.
Cast off.

MAKE UP

With centre of sleeves to shoulder seam, sew on sleeves. Join side and sleeve seams. Sew in zip.

SIMPLE JACKET hat and bootees

Ideal for the relatively inexperienced knitter, this simple garter stitch jacket has cuffs edged in a contrasting colour, plus matching bootees and a hat. There is also an accompanying throw on page 58. The bootees are shown in two different colourways, opposite and on page 81.

Materials

Debbie Bliss Cotton DK (100% cotton; 84m/91yd per 50g/1¾oz ball) DK (light worsted) weight yarn:

For the jacket:
  7(8:9) balls of shade Steel Blue (M)
  1 ball of shade Ecru (A)
Pair each of 3.75mm (US 5) and 4mm (US 6) knitting needles
6(7:7) buttons

For the bootees:
  1 ball of shade Ecru or Steel Blue(M)
  1 ball of shade Steel Blue or Ecru (A)
Pair 3.25mm (US 3) knitting needles

For the hat:
  1 ball of shade Ecru (M)
  1 ball of shade Steel Blue (A)
Pair 4mm (US 6) knitting needles

Measurements

Jacket

To fit age	6-9	9-12	12-24	months.
Actual measurements				
Chest	56	62	70	cm
	22	24½	27½	in
Length to shoulder	26	30	34	cm
	10¼	11¾	13½	in
Sleeve length (cuff turned back)	16	18	20	cm
	6¼	7	8	in

Hat

To fit age	6-9	9-12	12-24	months.

Bootees

To fit age		6-12 months.	

Tension

20 sts and 40 rows to 10cm/4in square over garter st (every row k) using 4mm (US 6) needles.

Abbreviations

See page 95.

JACKET

POCKET LININGS (MAKE 2)

With 4mm (US 6) needles and yarn M cast on 15(17:19) sts.
K 24(28:32) rows. Leave these sts on a holder.

BACK AND FRONTS

With 4mm (US 6) needles and yarn A cast on 112(124:140) sts.
K 1 row.
Cont in yarn M.
K 24(28:32) rows.

Place pockets

Next row K6(7:8), cast off 15(17:19) sts, k next 69(75:85) sts, cast off 15(17:19) sts, k to end.

Next row K6(7:8), k across sts of first pocket lining, k70(76:86) sts, k across sts of second pocket lining, k6(7:8).

Cont in straight in garter st until work measures 15(17:19)cm/6(6¾:7½)in from cast on edge, ending with a wrong side row.

Divide for back and fronts

Next row K28(31:35), leave these sts on a holder for right front, k next 56(62:70), leave these sts on a holder for back, k to end.

LEFT FRONT

Work straight on last set of 28(31:35) sts until front measures 22(25:28)cm/8¾(9¾:11)in from cast on edge, ending at neck edge.

Shape neck

Next row K6(7:8) sts, leave these sts on a safety pin, k to end.

Dec one st at neck edge on every row until 14(16:18) sts rem.

Work straight until front measures 26(30:34)cm/10¼(11¾:13½)in from cast on edge, ending at armhole edge.

Shape shoulder

Cast off.

BACK

With wrong side facing, rejoin yarn to next st.

Work straight until back measures same as Left Front to shoulder, ending with a wrong side row.

Shape shoulders

Cast off 14(16:18) sts at beg of next 2 rows.

Leave rem 28(30:34) sts on a spare needle.

RIGHT FRONT

With wrong side facing, rejoin yarn to next st, work to match Left Front, reversing all shapings.

SLEEVES

With 4mm (US 6) needles and yarn A cast on 32(34:38) sts.

K 1 row.

Cont in yarn M.

K 16 rows.

Change to 3.75mm (US 5) needles.

K 16 rows.

Change to 4mm (US 6) needles

Cont in garter st, inc one st at each end of the next and every foll 5th row until there are 48(56:64) sts.

Cont straight until sleeve measures 20(22:24)cm/8(8½:9½)in from cast on edge, ending with a wrong side row.

Cast off.

NECKBAND

Join shoulder seams.

With right side facing, using 3.75mm (US 5) needles and yarn A, k6(7:8) sts from safety pin, pick up and k12(14:16) sts up right front neck edge, k across 28(30:34) sts on back neck, pick up and k12(14:16) sts down left side of front neck, k6(7:8) sts from safety pin. 64(72:82) sts.

K 2 rows.

Cast off.

BUTTONBAND

With right side facing, using 3.75mm (US 5) needles and yarn A, pick up and k46(52:58) sts along left front edge.

K 2 rows.

Cast off.

BUTTONHOLE BAND

With right side facing, using 3.75mm (US 5) needles and yarn A, pick up and k46(52:58) sts along right front edge.

Buttonhole row K2(1:1) sts, [k2 tog, yf, k6(6:7) sts] 5(6:6) times, k2 tog, yf, k2(1:1).

K 1 row.

Cast off.

TO MAKE UP

Join sleeve seams, reversing seam on cuff for 4cm/1¾in. Sew in sleeves.

Sew on buttons.

BOOTEES

With 3.25mm (US 3) needles and yarn M, cast on 48 sts.

K 1 row.

1st row K1, yf, k22, yf, k2, yf, k22, yf, k1.

2nd and 4 foll alt rows K to end, working k1b into yf of previous row.

3rd row K2, yf, k23, yf, k2, yf, k23, yf, k2.

5th row K3, yf, k24, yf, k2, yf, k24, yf, k3.

60 sts.

6th row K to end, working k1b into yf of previous row.

K 6 rows.

Shape top

Next row K26, k3 tog, k2, k3 togb, k26.

K 1 row.

Next row K24, k3 tog, k2, k3 togb, k24.

K 1 row.

Next row K22, k3 tog, k2, k3 togb, k22.

K 1 row.

Next row K20, k3 tog, k2, k3 togb, k20.

K 1 row.

Next row K18, k3 tog, k2, k3 togb, k18.

K 1 row. 40 sts.

Next row K17, k2 tog, k2, skpo, k17.

K 1 row.

Next row K16, k2 tog, k2, skpo, k16.

K 1 row.

Cont in this way dec 2 sts on every alt row until 30 sts rem.

K 7 rows.

Next row K15, turn and k 4 rows.

Cont in yarn A.

K 1 row.

Cast off.

With right side facing, rejoin yarn M to rem sts, k to end.

K 4 rows.

Cont in yarn A.

K 1 row.

Cast off.

MAKE UP

Join seam, reversing seam on last 4 rows. Using yarn A, make pom-poms and sew to toes.

HAT

With 4mm (US 6) needles and yarn A, cast on 71(81:91) sts.

Starting with a k row work 6 rows st st.

Cont in yarn M.

Cont in garter st.

Work 36 rows.

1st dec row K1, [k2 tog, k8] 7(8:9) times.

K 1 row.

2nd dec row K1, [k2 tog, k7] 7(8:9) times.

K 1 row.

3rd dec row K1, [k2 tog, k6] 7(8:9) times.

K 1 row.

Cont to dec in this way until 15(17:19) sts rem.

Next row K1, [k2 tog] to end. 8(9:10) sts.

Break off yarn thread through rem sts, pull up and secure.

Join seam. Using yarn A, make a pom-pom and sew to crown.

TECHNIQUES

In this section you will find illustrations and explanations of the more complex techniques, such as colour and cable knitting, used in some of the patterns in this book.

Always read the instructions given on the knitting pattern as well as referring to the specific technique illustrated in this section, as there may be additional elements to be aware of.

WORKING FROM A CHART

Colour designs are usually illustrated with symbols or colours on a graph. Each square represents one stitch and one row. In the same way that you knit upwards from the bottom of your work, so you read the chart from the bottom row upwards.

In a repeated design the chart will show how many stitches are repeated across the row and there may be edge stitches either side of this repeat. The edge stitches are worked once at the beginning and end of the row and the repeat is worked as many times as necessary.

Unless otherwise stated, the first row of the chart is the first row of the colour pattern and is usually a knit row, which is followed by reading the chart from right to left. The second row is usually a purl row and for this the chart is read from left to right.

Individual motifs, such as the flower shown below, do not always start on a right side row, depending on where they are placed on the garment. If they start on a wrong side row, the first row of the chart is read from left to right.

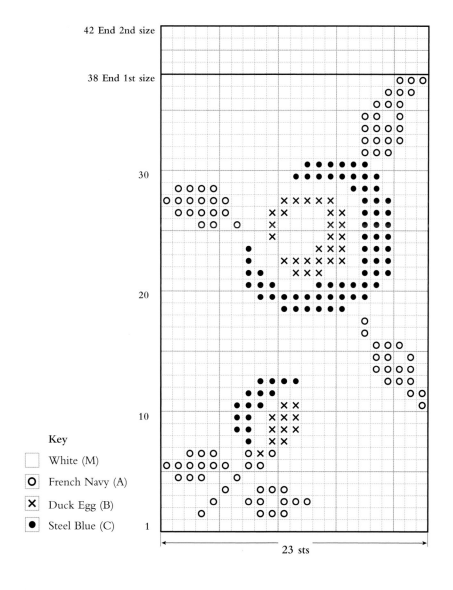

42 End 2nd size

38 End 1st size

30

20

10

1

Key

☐ White (M)

◯ French Navy (A)

✗ Duck Egg (B)

● Steel Blue (C)

23 sts

FAIR ISLE KNITTING

Stranding is used when the yarn not being used is left at the back of the work until needed. The loops formed by stranding are called 'floats' and it is important to ensure that they are not pulled too tightly when working the next stitch, as this will pull in your knitting. If the gap between the colours is more than four stitches the weaving in

method is preferable, as this prevents floats becoming too long and stopping the fabric having the right amount of elasticity. Many colour patterns will use both techniques and you should choose the one that is the most appropriate to a particular part of the design.

STRANDING

1 On a knit row, hold the first colour in your right hand and the second colour in your left hand. Knit the required number of stitches as usual with the first colour, carrying the second colour loosely across the wrong side of the work.

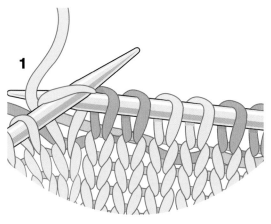

2 To knit a stitch in the second colour, insert the right hand needle into the next stitch then draw a loop through from the yarn held in the left hand, carrying the yarn in the right hand loosely across the wrong side until required.

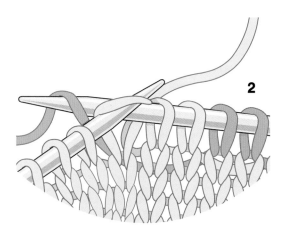

3 On a purl row, hold the yarns as for the knit rows. Purl the required number of stitches as usual with the first colour, carrying the second colour loosely across these stitches on the wrong side of the work.

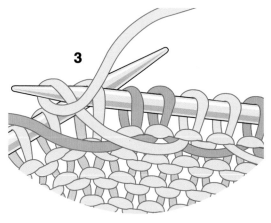

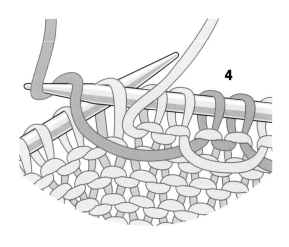

4 To purl a stitch in the second colour, insert the right hand needle into the next stitch then draw a loop through from the yarn held in the left hand, carrying the yarn in the right hand loosely across the wrong side until next required.

WEAVING

In weaving in, or knitting in, the floats are caught in by the working yarn on every third or fourth stitch. Weaving in on alternate stitches can distort stitches and alter the tension.

1 Insert the right hand needle into the stitch. Lay the contrast yarn over the point of the right hand needle then knit the stitch in the usual way, taking care not to knit in the contrast yarn.

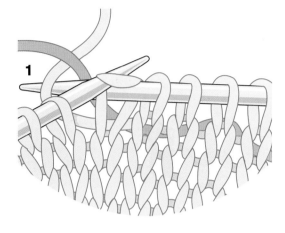

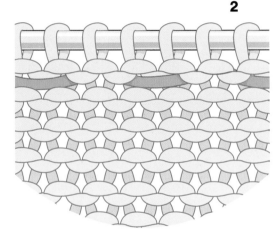

2 When you knit the next stitch, the contrast yarn will have been caught in. Use the same method to catch in the yarn on the purl rows.

A simple Fair Isle border on a moss stitch scarf.

The back of stranded and woven fabric can look very neat if the technique is worked carefully.

INTARSIA KNITTING

Intarsia is the name given to colour knitting where the pattern is worked in large blocks of colour at a time, requiring a separate length or ball of yarn for each area of colour, as the yarn must not be stranded at the back.

DIAGONAL COLOUR CHANGE WITH A SLANT TO THE LEFT

1 This illustration shows a colour change on the wrong side of the work.

Use separate lengths or balls of yarn for each block of colour. On a right side row, with the yarns at the back of the work, the crossing of colours at joins happens automatically because of the encroaching nature of the pattern. On a wrong side row, with the yarns at the front of the work, take the first colour over the second colour, drop it then pick up the second colour underneath the first colour thus crossing the two colours together.

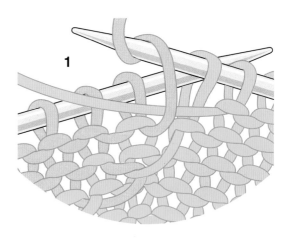

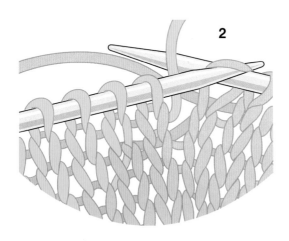

VERTICAL COLOUR CHANGE

3 This illustration shows a colour change on the wrong side of the work.

Use separate lengths or balls of yarn for each block of colour. Work in the first colour to the colour change, then drop the first colour, pick up the second colour underneath the first colour, crossing the two colours over before working the next stitch in the second colour. The first stitch after a colour change is worked firmly to avoid a gap forming between colours. This technique ensures that the yarns are crossed on every row and gives a neat vertical line between colours on the right side, and a vertical line of loops in each colour on the wrong side.

DIAGONAL COLOUR CHANGE WITH A SLANT TO THE RIGHT

2 This illustration shows a colour change on the right side of the work.

Use separate lengths or balls of yarn for each block of colour. On a right side row, with the yarns at the back of the work, take the first colour over the second colour, drop it then pick up the second colour underneath the first colour thus crossing the two colours over. On a wrong side row, with the yarns at the front of the work, the crossing of the two colours at the joins happens automatically because of the encroaching nature of the pattern.

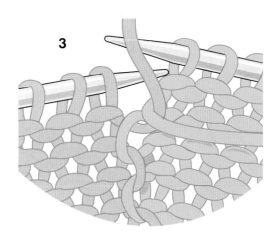

Intarsia is the perfect technique for knitting separated
motifs worked across the knitted fabric.

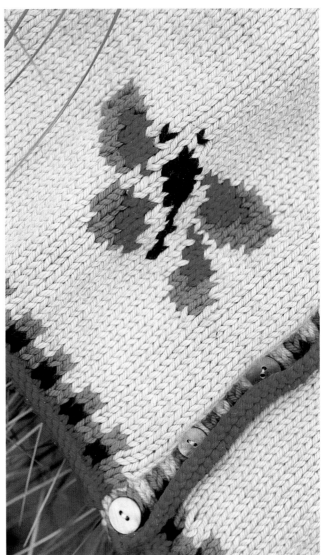

A good design touch is to use the same colours
for motifs and borders on a garment.

When working larger intarsia motifs do
not cut the lengths of yarn too short.

BASIC CABLE

Cables are made by crossing one group of stitches over another. The number of stitches that are crossed can vary to make larger and smaller cables, and the number of rows between each crossover can also vary. Once the basic cable technique has been mastered, it can be used to reproduce many pattern variations. The cable shown here is a basic four-stitch pattern in stocking stitch, worked on a reverse stocking stitch background. Where different cables are given in the patterns, use the same basic technique, but follow the instructions given with the pattern.

CABLE 4 FRONT (C4F)

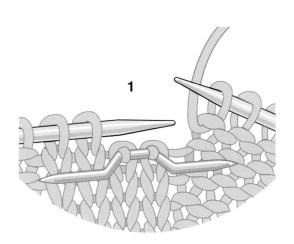

1 On a right side row, work to the position of the cable panel then slip the next two stitches onto the cable needle, leaving it at the front of the work.

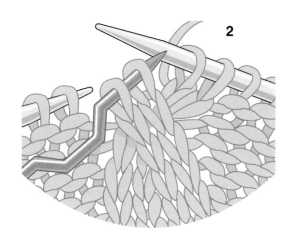

2 Working behind the cable needle, knit the next two stitches from the left hand needle.

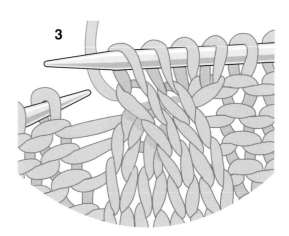

3 Now knit the two stitches from the cable needle to produce a cable that crosses to the left.
For a cable 4 back (C4B) leave the stitches on the cable needle at the back of the work.

KNITTING WITH BEADS

Beads can be sewn onto your finished knitting or knitted in. When knitted in the beads 'hang' very slightly on the surface of the fabric from the strand of yarn at the front of the slipped stitch.

Most patterns specify the number of beads to be threaded on to each ball of yarn. If not, thread up one ball with more beads than you will need, then count the number used after completing that ball. It is important to thread on the correct number of beads (or more) before beginning to knit; once

the ball is started you will not be able to add more unless you unwind the ball and add them from the other end, or break the yarn.

The knitted fabric should be fairly firm or the beads may slip through to the wrong side, and the additional weight of the beads may drag a loosely knitted garment out of shape. The beads should be a suitable weight for the yarn and must have a large enough hole for double-thickness yarn to pass through.

1 If the yarn and needle are thin enough you can thread them straight through the beads. If not, use the method shown here.
Fold a length of sewing cotton in half and thread both ends through a sewing needle. Thread the end of the yarn through the loop in the sewing cotton and fold it back on itself. Thread beads along the needle, down the sewing cotton and onto the yarn until you have the number of beads on the yarn that your pattern requires.

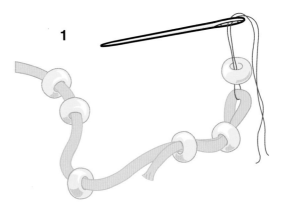

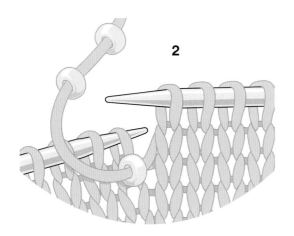

2 On a right side row, knit to the position of the beaded stitch. Bring the yarn forward to the front of the work and push a bead down the yarn close to the last stitch so that it lies over the front of the next stitch.

3 Slip the next stitch purlwise, leaving the bead in front of the slipped stitch. Take the yarn to the back and continue the work as normal.

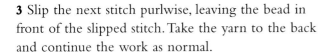

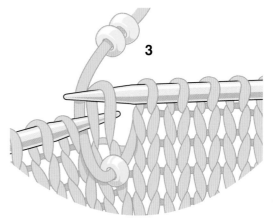

EMBROIDERY

Knitted fabric is a good base for simple embroidery, as you can use the horizontal and vertical lines as guides in placing the stitches. Choose your embroidery thread or yarn carefully; if it is too thin it can disappear into the knitted fabric, and if it is too thick it can distort the fabric. Before you start stitching, fasten the end of the thread on the reverse of the fabric or leave a loose end to weave in later. To follow a specific embroidery pattern, you can trace the design onto tissue paper and pin this in place on the knitted fabric. Embroider through the paper and fabric and then pull away the paper. The following stitches are ones that I like to use and those that are worked on the Embroidered Dress on page 8.

FRENCH KNOTS

Bring the needle and thread up through the knitted fabric and then wind the thread twice around the needle. Keeping the thread taut around the needle, take the needle back down through the fabric very close to where it first emerged. Bring the needle up again in the right position for the next knot.

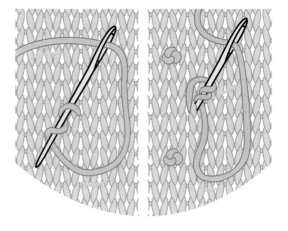

LAZY DAISY

Bring the needle and thread up through the knitted fabric. Take it down through the fabric in the same place and bring the tip of it up through the fabric a short distance away. Loop the thread under the needle and then pull the needle right through. Take the needle down through the fabric over the loop to secure it in place. Bring the needle up again in the right position for the next lazy daisy stitch.

SATIN STITCH

Work parallel stitches, close together, bringing the needle up and taking it down through the knitted fabric on the edges of the design. Do not pull the thread tightly or you will distort the fabric.

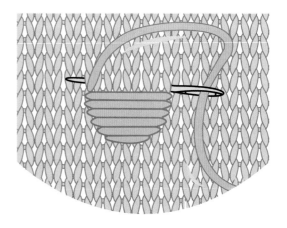

The diagram above shows where to place the embroidery stitches to create the floral swag shown at the top (see also page 8).

MAKING UP

'Making up' is the term used to describe finishing your garment. Sloppy sewing up can ruin a beautifully knitted garment, but by using the methods shown here you can create virtually invisible seams. Check the yarn ball band to see if there are any special pressing instructions you must follow before you start sewing.

JOINING A SIDE SEAM ON STOCKING STITCH FABRIC (MATTRESS STITCH)

Right sides up, lay the pieces to be joined flat and edge to edge. Thread a blunt-pointed needle with yarn and attach the yarn to the back of one side. Bring the needle out to the front between the edge stitch and the second stitch in the first row. Insert the needle between the edge stitch and the second stitch in the first row on the opposite side. Pass the needle under the loops of one or two rows, then bring it back through to the front. Insert the needle into the hole that the last stitch came out of on the first side and pass it under the loops of one or two rows to emerge in the same place as on the opposite side. Repeat this zigzag action, always taking the needle under the strands that correspond exactly to those on the other side, taking care not to miss any rows. After a few stitches pull up the yarn thus closing the seam. Make sure that the seam is at the same tension as the rest of the fabric.

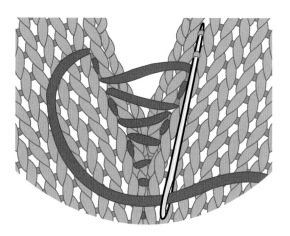

JOINING A SIDE SEAM ON SINGLE RIB

When joining two ribbed sections together, it is best to take in only half a stitch on either side, so that when the two pieces are drawn together one complete knit stitch in formed along the seam. Join the seam in the same way as for stocking stitch but pass the needle under the loop of one row at a time rather than two. To join double rib, use the same method, but take in a whole stitch, as with mattress stitch, for the least visible seam.

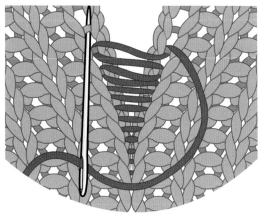

JOINING TWO CAST OFF EDGES

1 Two cast off edges can be joined together in a similar way as for a side seam. Bring the needle out in the centre of the first stitch below the casting off stitch on one side. Insert the needle in the centre of the first stitch on the opposite side and bring it out in the centre of the next stitch.

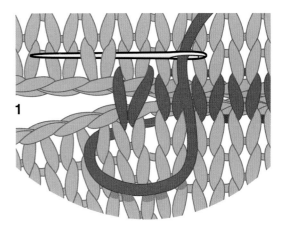

2 Return to the first stitch and insert the needle in the centre of the first stitch, bring it out in the centre of the next stitch.

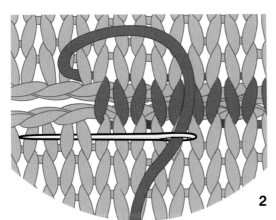

Wonderfully neat, professional-looking seams can be achieved using proper joining stitches.

BASIC INFORMATION

NOTES

In the patterns figures for larger sizes are given in round ( ) brackets. Where only one size is given this means that it applies to all sizes.

Work the figures in the square [ ] brackets the number of times stated. Where 0 appears no stitches or rows are worked for this size.

The quantities of yarn stated are based on average requirements and are therefore approximate. A small variation in tension can alter the amount of yarn you use so it is important to work a tension square before you start your project.

My patterns quote the actual size of the finished garment rather than the bust/chest of the wearer and this will tell you how much ease the design has, whether it is close fitting or generously sized. Check these measurements before you knit; if want to make up the design with more or less ease you may have to knit up a larger or smaller size.

YARNS

The following descriptions of the yarns used in this book are a guide to the yarn weight and type. Turn to page 96 for stockist information.

Debbie Bliss Baby Cashmerino: a 55% merino wool, 33% acrylic, 12% cashmere lightweight DK (sport) yarn. Approximately 125m (137yd) per 50g (1¾oz) ball.

Debbie Bliss Cotton DK: a 100% pure cotton double knitting (light worsted) yarn. Approximately 84m (91yd) per 50g (1¾oz) ball.

Always try to buy the yarn quoted in the pattern, but if you do use a substitute, buy a yarn with the same metreage and wherever possible, the same fibre content. It is essential to compare the metreage as a ball of yarn that weighs the same may be a different length, so you may need to buy more or less yarn.

Also check dye lots. Buy the full amount of yarn quoted, checking that all the balls are from the same dye lot. If you buy yarn in small amounts you may find that the retailer has received a new dye lot and the colour may be subtly different.

TENSION

Each pattern in the book specifies a tension: the number of stitches and rows per centimetre or inch that should be obtained with the given needles, yarn and stitch pattern. However eager you are to start a pattern you should always make time to work a tension square to avoid disappointment when you have finished the garment. Tighter or looser tension can make the difference between a smaller or larger garment than the one you wanted and alter the yarn amounts you use.

To knit a tension square, use the same yarn, needles, and stitch pattern as those quoted in the tension note, which appears before the main part of the pattern. Knit a sample at least 13cm/5in square. Smooth out the finished sample on a flat surface, but make sure you do not stretch it. To check the stitch tension, place a ruler horizontally on the sample and mark 10cm/4in with pins. To check the row tension place the ruler vertically on the sample and mark 10cm/4in with pins. Count the number of stitches and rows between the pins.

If you have more stitches and rows than that quoted in the tension note then your knitting is too tight and you need to try again using a larger needle. If you have less stitches and rows, your knitting is too loose and you need to try again using a smaller needle. As a lot of patterns quote the length in measurement rather than rows, it is more important that you achieve the correct stitch tension.

ABBREVIATIONS

Some knitting terms may be unfamiliar to readers. The list below gives the general abbreviations that are used throughout the book. More specific abbreviations are explained at the beginning of the relevant pattern.

alt = alternate

beg = beginning

cont = continu(e)(ing)

cm = centimetre(s)

dec = decrease(ing)

foll = follow(s)(ing)

g = gram(mes)

in = inch(es)

inc = increase one stitch by working into the front and back of the next stitch

k = knit

k1b = knit through back of loop

m1(p) = make one by picking up the loop between the stitch just worked and the next stitch and knitting (purling) into the back of it.

M= main (colour)

m = metre(s)

mm = millimetre(s)

patt = pattern

p = purl

p1b = purl through back of loop

psso = pass slipped stitch over

rem = remain(ing)

rep = repeat(ing)

skpo = slip one, knit one, pass slipped stitch over

sl = slip

st(s) = stitch(es)

st st = stocking (stockinette) stitch

tog = together

togb = together through back of loops

yb = yarn back

yd = yard(s)

yf = yarn forward

yon = yarn over needle

yrn = yarn around needle

CARE OF GARMENTS

Check the ball band for washing instructions. All the yarns used are machine washable on a delicate cycle, although personally I still prefer to handwash my handknits as much as possible. Dry them flat on a towel, patting them into shape. Do not dry them near direct heat such as a radiator. It is better to store your handknits loosely folded to let them 'breathe'.

UK KNITTING TERMS

The following terms may be unfamiliar to US readers

UK terms	US terms
Aran	worsted
ball band	yarn wrapper
cast off	bind off
double knitting yarn	light worsted
make up (garment)	finish (garment)
moss stitch	seed stitch
rib	ribbing
stocking stitch	stockinette stitch
tension	gauge
yarn forward	yarn over
yarn over needle	yarn over
yarn round needle	yarn over

ACKNOWLEDGEMENTS

This book would not have been possible without the dedication of the following:

Most importantly, the knitters, who always work with impossible deadlines:
Dorothy Bayley, Cynthia Brent, Pat Church, Jaqui Dunt, Janet Fagan, Penny Hill, Shirley Kennet, Maisie Lawrence, Beryl Salter and Frances Wallace.

Jane Bunce, for her commitment to all my projects, and the butterfly cardigan and bag, and Jane Crowfoot, for the lovely embroidery and the tartan beaded bag.

Craig Fordham, the photographer, for the beautiful photography and Rob, his assistant, for his uncanny impersonations of owls and Toby Jugs.

Marilyn Wilson, the pattern checker, for her hard work and thorough checking.

Penny Hill, for pattern compiling.

Kate Haxell, the project manager, for her support and making it all work.

Sammi Bell, for the lovely styling.

Georgina Harris, managing editor, for her enthusiasm.

Cindy Richards and Mark Collins, for initiating the project.

Heather Jeeves, for being a terrific agent.

The models, for making the book such fun to work on: Aggie, Brandon, Caitlin, Charlie, Harry, Lavinia, Nou, Scarlet, Somerset, Summer and Tally.

STOCKISTS

Debbie Bliss yarns are available exclusively from LoveCrafts, and can be shipped worldwide:
lovecrafts.com